Peter Alpho

Disciplina Clericalis

(English translation)

From the fifteenth century Worcester Cathedral

Manuscript F. 172

Peter Alphonse's,

William Henry Hulme

Alpha Editions

This edition published in 2019

ISBN : 9789353891541

Design and Setting By
Alpha Editions
email - alphaedis@gmail.com

Western Reserve University

BULLETIN

VOL. XXII   MAY, 1919   No. 3

LITERARY SECTION

CLEVELAND, OHIO

1919

Issued Bimonthly by
WESTERN RESERVE UNIVERSITY
10940 Euclid Avenue, Cleveland

THE WESTERN RESERVE UNIVERSITY BULLETIN
LITERARY SECTION
PUBLISHED BIMONTHLY BY THE UNIVERSITY

General Editor: PROFESSOR WILLIAM HENRY HULME

WESTERN RESERVE STUDIES VOL. I, NO. 5.

This series of studies will, it is hoped, include in easily accessible form some of the valuable results of the researches undertaken by members of the various faculties, as well as, by Alumni of Western Reserve University. All serious students connected with any department of the University are therefore cordially invited to submit to the Editor pieces of original work which they desire to have published. If the piece of work represents a genuine contribution to the particular field in which it lies, it will be printed in the *Bulletin*. But only such contributions will be accepted for publication. Unfortunately, for some years to come it is feared, the annual issue of these studies will have to be limited to the May number (considerably increased in size when necessary), unless a special fund can be obtained for this purpose.

In order that the contributions from every department of the University may be sure of 'specialist' and fair editorial treatment, an Editorial Committee will assist the General Editor of the *Bulletin* in passing upon articles, the contents of which may be unfamiliar to him. To this end the following members of the University Faculty have kindly consented to serve on the Committee: Professors Arbuthnot (of the department of Economics), Bourne (of the department of History), Emerson (of the department of English), Herrick (of the department of Biology), and Todd (of the department of Anatomy).

WESTERN RESERVE UNIVERSITY BULLETIN

NEW SERIES

VOL. XXII   MAY, 1919   No. 3

LITERARY SECTION SUPPLEMENT

WESTERN RESERVE STUDIES, VOL. I, No. 5

PETER ALPHONSE'S

DISCIPLINA CLERICALIS

(ENGLISH TRANSLATION)

FROM

The Fifteenth Century Worcester Cathedral Manuscript F. 172

— Ms

BY

WILLIAM HENRY HULME, PH. D.

Professor of English

CONTENTS

PREFACE

The present edition of Peter Alphonse's *Disciplina Clericalis* is intended to be a preliminary study for the fuller treatment of the subject which I promised several years ago to give in one of the volumes of the publications of the Early English Text Society, but which has not yet been completed. At the outbreak of the war I was in England reading and collecting materials from every possible source. But this work, necessarily broken off in the very midst of things, could not be taken up again during the last five years: so the matter rests where it was left in the summer of 1914. I hope, however, that it will be possible to resume the necessary search after analogues and originals of the various tales of the collection in both ancient and mediaeval literatures at no distant date and to carry it to a successful conclusion in the prospective EETS edition. The edition which is now presented will in the nature of things reach only a limited number of students and readers. But it will be of great practical value, I hope, to all who are interested in the study of mediaeval folk-tales generally, as well as of Peter Alphonse's collection in particular, since it offers a convenient and, it is intended, reliable text of the Middle English version as a much needed basis for all further editorial work.

My interest in the *Disciplina* began some years ago while I was engaged in collecting materials for the EETS edition of the Middle English *Harrowing of Hell and Poetical Gospel of Nicodemus*. But the identification of this unheralded, unrubicated piece in the Worcester Cathedral Ms. was immediately due to the interest and suggestion of Mr. J. A. Herbert (at that time Assistant in the Department of Manuscripts, now Keeper of Manuscripts, in the British Museum), to whose kindness and courtesy I have so frequently been a debtor in recent years.

Since the EETS edition will be amply provided with Introduction, Notes, and Glossarial Vocabulary, in addition to, in all probability, a reprint of the Latin version of the Cambridge University Library Ms. li, 6, 11 in parallel columns with the Middle English, the "critical apparatus" has been for the most part omitted from this edition. Besides, the lack of space in these publications makes it incumbent on the editor to compress the introductory materials into the smallest practicable compass. No attempt has accordingly been made to treat any phase of the broad subject exhaustively,—not even to give a full bibliography of the literature on the subject. But the titles of a few of the most important works of both a general and a specific character are given, in which the eager student will probably find virtually all the literature on the *Disciplina Clericalis,* as well as on mediaeval tales and fables, recorded.

I have tried to give, in the proper connection (printed in solid type in the text, or occasionally in the footnotes) free English translations from the original Latin for all the *lacunae* of any consequence in the Middle English text, whether they occur as parts of, or complete, individual tales, or as omissions from the connecting dialogues. In making the translations I have had the generous assistance for corrective purposes of Professor Platner of the department of Latin, which enabled me, I trust, to retain the sense and something of the interest of the original without a superfluity of errors. One missing tale has been supplied from the Middle English *Alphabet of Tales* (No. VII), another from Caxton's *Aesop* (No. XII).

In the text an effort has been made to reduce correction and emendation to a minimum, and the essential features of the manuscript have, it is hoped, been preserved. Spelling and capitalization have been altered only when it was felt necessary for the understanding of the text. The punctuation is, on the other hand, entirely my own, that of the Ms. being such as would frequently confuse the reader and convey a wholly false meaning. The abbreviations of the manuscript have not been indicated by the usual italic type; they are comparatively few in number and include, in the main *-er, -is, n* (*m*), and *u,*—but all of them only occasionally. And even a large percentage of the abbreviations present occur at the ends of lines. Isolated instances of the early English thorn (for *th*), which occur mostly at the ends of lines, have been printed as *th*. Additions to the Ms. text are indicated by brackets.

In general, what was said about the word forms and language of 'The Mending of Life' (see *Western Reserve Studies.* vol. I, No. 4, p. 27f) applies equally well to those features of the *Disciplina Clericalis.* New word-forms occur from time to time which the exigencies of translation required and for the same reason the sentence structure would probably often be found different from that of 'The Mending of Life'. But these peculiarities will receive full treatment in the EETS edition.

INTRODUCTION

I

Peter Alphonse,* the author of the popular mediaeval collection of oriental folk tales or exempla, known as *Disciplina Clericalis*, was, according to his own testimony, born at Huesca in the kingdom of Aragon in the year 1062.† He was a Jew by birth and was known before his conversion by the name of Rabbi Moses Sephardi, or Moses the Spaniard. He was baptized under the name 'Petrus Alphonsus,'—the first part of the name due to the apostle on whose birthday the event occurred, the second part deriving from Alphonsus I†, "the glorious emperor of Spain who was my spiritual father and who received me at the baptismal font."* He was according to Söderhjelm† one of the many Jewish intellectuals of the Middle Ages who served as intermediaries between oriental and occidental culture.

A few years after his conversion he published his *Dialogi*—or *Dialogus contra Judaeos**—in which the Christian Peter defends the doctrines of Christianity against the attacks of Moses the Jew (representing the attitude of the author before his conversion as well as that of the orthodox Jews of his time).

It was probably not far from the same time that the *Disciplina Clericalis* was written. The author had at least already become a Christian,—a fact fully established by the Prolog of the *Disciplina*, which begins: "Petir Alfons, seruaunt of Jesus Christ maker of this book," and, "I return thanks to God who is the first without beginning;" and the author closes the Prolog with, "May the omnipo-

---

*This seems to be the natural modern form of the second part of the name; though such forms as Aldefunsi, Adelfonsi, Amphulsi, Alfunsi, Alfonsi, Alphunsus, Alfonsus, Anfonsus, Anfulsus, etc., occur, and out text has Alfons. Cf. Hilka and Söderhjelm *Die Disciplina Clericalis des Petrus Alfunsi.* Heidelberg, 1911. Sammlung mittellateinischer Texte, hrsg von Alfons Hilka. No. I, Introd. p. vii.

†See Migne, *Patrologia Latina,* vol. 157, col. 537-38. In the preface to the *Dialogi,* when speaking of his conversion to Christianity and his baptism, he says: "This (i. e. his baptism) happened in the year 1106 after the nativity of our Lord and in the 44th year of my life, in the month of July on the birthday of the apostles Peter and Paul. Hoc autem factum est anno a nativitate Domini millesimo centesimo sexto, aetatis meae anno quadragesimo quarto, mense Julio, die natalis apostolorum Petri et Pauli.

†See Söderhjelm, *op. cit.;* but Labouderie speaks of him (Migne, *op. cit.* col. 531) as "Alphonse VI, king of Castille and Leon."

*Cf. Migne, *op. cit.* col. 538: Fuit autem pater meus spiritualis Alfunsus, gloriosus Hispaniae imperator, qui me de sacro fonte suscepit, quare nomen ejus praefato nomini meo apponens, Petrus Alfunsi mihi nomen imposui.
†*Op. cit.* p. vii.

*Though the work is so designated by Söderhjelm, Migne *op. cit.* col. 531, also cols. 535-6 and 537-8, always refers to it as Dialogi. Labouderie speaks of an edition printed in Cologne in 1536 under the title, Dialogi lectu dignissimi, in quibus impiae Judaeorum opiniones, et. cet.; the preface begins: Petri Alphonsi ex Judaeo Christiani Dialogi; and the discussion itself has the following title (Migne, cols. 537-38): *Incipit Dialogus Petri cognomento Alphonsi, ex Judaeo Christiani et Moysi Judaei.*

tent God be my helper in this work." That is to say, the *Disciplina Clericalis* was written (or compiled) not long after the beginning of the 12th century. It is accordingly the earliest complete collection of oriental tales made known to the western world, and one which enjoyed great popularity and very wide distribution in the literatures of western nations during the twelfth, thirteenth, fourteen, and fifteen centuries. One might even say without exaggeration, that the *Disciplina Clericalis* of Peter Alphonse not only made known for the first time a considerable number of those tales which were soon to become the most popular of western literatures, but that it inaugurated in all probability that later universally popular kind of prose fiction called the *Novella*. And though the *exemplum* had for several centuries been employed by the church fathers for illustrating and pointing their sermons, there was probably no collection of exampla, whether culled from sermons of the fathers or derived from other sources, in existence at the time the *Disciplina* was composed*. In Peter Alphonse's work, indeed, the exemplum has taken on much more the character of an independent tale, unconnected with any moralizing plan or distinctly religious purpose, than had hitherto been the case.

Nevertheless, there is a decided thread of moral purpose running through the *Disciplina Clericalis,* which shows itself clearly, if not in the individual tales themselves, at least in the dialogues of varying length which, in the original Latin, always serve as connecting links between the successive exempla. But the moral, didactic features of the collection seem to be, either with or without the consciousness of the author, already of less consequence—certainly of less interest—to the reader than the tales themselves in their purely literary and artistic aspects. As compared with the early sermons, therefore, illustrated by isolated exempla, in which the moral and

---

*On the origin and development of the 'exemplum' see J. A. Mosher, *The Exemplum in the Early Religious and Didactic Literature of England.* Columbia Univ. Studies in English. New York, 1911, chap. I. In the thorough study of the *Disciplina Clericalis* which ·the present writer ˙hopes to make in the near future in connection with the EETS edition, the questions concerning the origins and analogues of the collection as a. whole, as well as of each individual exemplum, will receive detailed consideration. Suggestions regarding the similarity between the *Disciplina Clericalis* and earlier Hebrew treatises will˙ be found in '*The Path of Good Men;* ɑ collection of parental instructions to children by authors distinguished in Israel for wisdom and learning, viz.: Rabbi Judah ben Saul Aben Tibbon, for his son, Rabbi Samuel Aben Tibben. The illustrious Rabbi Moses Maimonides, for his son, Rabbi Abraham; being their Last Will for the Instruction of Mankind, etc. Edited from Manuscripts in the Bodleian Library, Oxford, accompanied by an English Translation.' By Hirsch Edelman. London 1852. Moreover, Victor Chauvin's *Bibĺographiє des Ouvrages Arabes ou Relatifs aux Arabes publies dans l' Europe chretienne de 1810 à 1885,* vol. (or Part) ix. Liège et Leipzig 1905, is a wonderful storehouse of information of every sort pertaining to the originals, analogues, and the history of the *Disciplina.* Much valuable information and numerous references to the literature on the subject will also be found in *The Seven Sages of Rome.* Edited by Killis Campbell, Boston, Ginn & Co., 1907. 'Introduction;' also in *Middle English Humorous Tales in Verse.* Edited by George H. McKnight, Boston, D. C. Heath &Co. 1913. 'Introduction' and 'Bibliography' (pp. 81-91).

religious purpose is the all important thing, the *Disciplina Clericalis* has inverted the order of human interests and taken a remarkable step in the direction of the inauguration of a wholly new species of prose literature.

II.

Recent studies of the *Disciplina*, in its original Latin form, have demonstrated one fact very clearly which earlier efforts had already made probable: that this work was one of the most popular and widely distributed treatises in the literatures of the Middle Ages* Hilka and Söderhjelm have described and classified sixty-three different manuscripts of the Latin versions of Peter Alphonse's collection, dating from the 12th century to the 16th, which they found in various libraries of England and the continent. Moreover it has long been known that French translations and adaptations of the *Disciplina* began to be made very early,—one version even in the last years of the 12th and another in the 13th century. These are poetical versions, one of which was published for the first time in the year 1760 by the French scholar Barbazan under the title *Le Castoiement d'un Père á son Fils*. A new edition of this version was published by Méon in vol. ii of his *Fabliaux et Contes des Poètes François des xi, xii, xiii, xiv, et xv Siècles* nouvelle edition. Paris 1808. A French prose translation was also made as early as the end of the 13th century, for one of the Mss. of this translation belongs to the beginning of the 14th century, and another to the middle of the 15th*. In addition to these French versions there are known to be Icelandic, Italian, German, Spanish, and English translations or adaptations of the whole, or a part, of the *Disciplina Clericalis*, all belonging, it seems, to the period of the Middle Ages†. But we only have space here for a brief account of English versions other than that of the Worc. Cath. Libr. Ms. F. 172. The results of the

†See the exhaustive comparative study of the Latin Manuscript versions by Alfons Hilka and Werner Söderhjelm in the *Acta Societatis Scientiarum Fennicae*, Tom. xxxviii, No. 4; *Petri Alfonsi Disciplina Clericalis*. I. Lateinischer Text Helsingfors, 1911. Introduction, pp. i-xxix. Part II, which appeared in 1912, contains the *Französischer Prosatext*; and as planned, Part III contains two French poetical versions, and Part IV a discussion of the distribution and influence of the *Disciplina Clericalis* in the literatures of the western world. Parts III-IV have not been accessible to me. Söderhjelm's 'Introduction 'to the smaller edition of the Disciplina—No. 1 in the Sammlung mittellateinischer Texte (referred to in this edition by the designation 'Söderhjelm,' while the larger Latin edition is referred to as 'I, 1, 2, etc.' or as 'Hilka and Söderhjelm')· is important in this connection. For there he gives a list of the important translations of the *Disciplina* in the different languages of the world, as well as of the books about it.

*See Hilka and Söderhjelm op. cij. II, Einleitung p. i ff. On p. x of the 'Introduction' there is a description of a Catalanian version, the Ms. of which is said to belong to the 16th century.

†Cf. Söderhjelm, op. cit. for more details regarding these various translations.

study of the influence which Peter Alphonse's work exerted on mediaeval literature, as shown by quotations of individual tales or by other references to it, can not yet be presented. This point has been treated briefly by Söderhjelm, as quoted above. It is, however, worth noting that numerous collections of exempla and sermons, such as those of Jacques de Vitry*, Albertano da Brescia, Odo of Cheriton, Étienne de Bourbon, Nicholas Bozon, Robert Holcot, Alphabetum Narrationum, Gesta Romanorum, etc., etc., from the 13-15 centuries, contain adaptations and quotations from Peter Alphonse in profusion.

Thirteen tales of the collection are included in the 15th century English version of the 'Alphabet of Tales'† and fourteen were printed by William Caxton in his *Book of the Subtyl Historyes and Fables of Esope,* which he himself tells us "were translated out of Frensshe into Englysshe . . . . . at Westmynstre in the yere of oure Lorde MCCCCLXXXIII.*" This book of Caxton is almost a literal translation of Jules de Machault's *Livre des subtilles Hystoires et Fables de Esope,* translatees de Latin en François, etc., in the year 1483[2]. Machault in turn made a comparatively free translation of Steinhöwels *Aesop,* and apparently from the Latin compilation arranged by Steinhöwel himself[3], rather than from his German version. Caxton follows Machault in omitting the last two of Steinhöwel's fifteen[4] tales of 'Adelfonso' from his translation. They all three also include one tale—No. xii—which is not in any

---

*Ed. Crane; cf. Herbert, *Catalogue of Romances in the Department of Manuscripts in the British Museum,* vol. iii, London, 1910, p. 1 ff.

†Ed. by Mary. M. Banks for the EETS vols. 126-127 (1904-1905). As the third volume has not yet appeared "a definite attribution of authorship" of the original *Alphabetum Narrationum,* formerly ascribed to Étienne de Besançon, must continue to wait. Cf. Banks, vol. 127, introductory 'note.'

*The book is a large folio Black Letter, profusely illustrated, and it contains some 210 pages of the Fables of Aesop, about 30 of the Fables of Auyon, and 18-20 pages of the Fables of "Poge the Florentyn," besides those of Peter Alphonse. In the epilogue to the book (ff. 142-142b) Caxton gives 1484 instead of 1483 as the date of printing: "And here with I fynysshe this book, translated and emprynted by me William Caxton at Westmynstre in thabbey; and fynysshed the xxvi daye of March, the yere of oure Lord MCCCCLXXXIIII, and the fyrst yere of the regne of Kyng Richard the Thyrdde." It is therefore evident that the translation was begun in the year 1483 and finished near the beginning of the following year, 'Old Style' of course. This book was re-edited with an interesting 'Introduction' and a 'Glossary' by Joseph Jacobs for David Nutt in 1889; *'The Fables of Aesop,* as first printed by William Caxton in 1484, with those of Avian, Alfonso and Poggio, 2 vols., London, 1889.'

[2] According to Söderhjelm, *op. cit.* p. xiv, though Oesterly says (*Steinhöwels Aesop,* hrsg. von Hermann Oesterley, Bibl. d. litt. Vereins in Stuttgart, Bd. 117, Tübingen 1873, Einleitung, p. 3): "The French translation of Julien Macho appeared first in the year 1484 and was reprinted at least ten times in the next fifty years."

[3] Oesterley *op. cit.* p. 2: "Steinhöwel was not only the translator of it, *i. e.* the Aesop of Planudes—Rimicius, etc. . . . . . but also the original compiler of the work which immediately on its publication became one of the most popular of the early printed books in the continent; besides the translation of Machault and indirectly, of Caxton, a Dutch translation of Steinhöwel's compilation was published in 1485, an Italian one by Tuppo in 1485 (Söderhjelm p. xiv), a Bohemian one in 1487, and later versions in both Spanish and Catalanian.

[4] In reality 16, for he merges the first two tales: (1) 'The Half Friend,' (2) 'The Perfect Friend' into one, in which he is followed by both Machault and Caxton.

oi the known manuscript versions of the original *Disciplina Clericalis*. Caxton designates this tale as follows: 'The xii fable is of a blynd man and of his wyf.' In Steinhöwel's compilation[5] the Latin title is, 'De ceco et eius uxore ac rivali;' the German, 'Von dem blinden und synem wyb.' Machault has, according to the Black Letter edition (without date) which belongs in the British Museum, 'La xii fable dun aueugle et de sa femme.' Now since Hilka and Söderhjelm do not mention this tale as being in any one of the 63 Mss. of the Latin versions of the *Disciplina Clericalis* which they have so carefully described and collated, it is not improbable that Steinhöwel incorrectly attributed this tale to Peter Alphonse (or one of his sources had done it) in gathering the materials for his compilation. The tale falls immediately after that of 'The Old Procuress with the Weeping Bitch'—one of the most popular of Peter Alphonse's collection—which is No. xiii of the original as arranged by Hilka and Söderhjelm,[6] and immediately before the story of 'The King's Tailor and his Servants'—No. xx of the Hilka-Söderhjelm edition and xviii of the earlier edition as reprinted by Migne (*op cit.* cols. 693-694.) On account the interest of the tale and for the sake of giving the reader an opportunity to compare the English of the Worc. version with that of Caxton (both being probably of about the same date) I reprint it herewith complete according to the original edition.

III.

The Blind Man Deceived by His Wife.

There was sometyme a blynd man whiche had a fayre wyf, of the whiche he was much Jalous. He kepte her so that she myght not goo nowher, for euer (Jacobs 'ewer') he had her by the hand. And after that she was enamoured of a gentil felawe, they coude not fynde the maner ne no place for to fulfylle theyr wyll. But notwithstandyng the woman whiche was subtyle and Ingenyous counceylled to her frende that he shold come in to her hows and that he shold entre in to (Jacobs omits 'to') the gardyn, and that there he shold clymme vpon a pere tree. And he did as she told hym.

And when they had made theyr enterpryse, the woman came ageyne in to the hows and sayd to her husbond: "My frend, I praye yow that ye wylle go in to our gardyn for to disporte (Jacobs 'despose') vs a lytel whyle there." Of the whiche prayer the blynd man was wel content and sayd to his wyf: "Wel my good frend, I

---

[5] Oesterley, p. 326ff.

[6] But No. xi in the earlier editions of Labouderie (Paris, 1824) and Schmitt (Berlin 1827.)

will wel; lete vs go thyder." And as they were vnder the pere tree she sayd to her husband: "My frende, I praye the to lete me goo vpon the pere tre, and I shalle gader for vs bothe some fayre peres." "Wel my frend," sayd the blynd man, "I wylle wel and graunt therto." And when (f. 132ᵇ) she was vpon the tree, the yong man begannn (sic) to shake the pere tree at one syde and the yonge woman at the other syde. And (Jacobs repeats 'and') as the blynd man herd thus hard shake the pere tree and the noyse whiche they made, he sayd to them: "Ha! a euylle woman, how be it that I see hit not, neuertheles I fele and vnderstande hit well. But I praye to the goddes that' they vouchesauf to sende me my syght ageyne." And as soone as he had made his prayer, Iupiter rendryd to hym his syght ageyn. And whanne he sawe that pagent vpon the pere tree he sayd to his wyf: "Ha! vnhappy woman, I shalle neuer haue no Ioye with the." And bycause that the yonge woman was redy in speche and malycious she ansuerd forthwith to her husbond: "My frend, thow arte wel beholden and bounden to me, for bycause and for the loue the gooddes haue restored to the thy syght; wherof I thanke alle the goddes and goddesses whiche haue enhaunced and herd my prayer. For I desyryng moche that thow myght see me cessed neuer day ne nyght to pray them that they (Jacobs 'theye') wold rendre to the thy syghte. Wherfore the goddesse Venus vysybly shewed herself to me and sayd that yf I wold doo (Jacobs omits) somme playsyr (Jacobs 'playsyre') to the sayd yonge man, she shold restore to the thy syght. And thus I am cause of it." And thenne the good man sayd to her: "My ryght dere wyf and good frende, I remercye and thanke yow gretely; for ryght ye haue and I grete wronge."

IV.

The Middle English version now first published as a whole[7] is preserved in the Worc. Cath. Libr. Ms. F. 172,[8] which probably originated in the latter half of the 15th century. The *Disciplina Clericalis* is number 15 in the order of the contents of the Ms. and is contained in ff. 118ᵇ—138. The piece begins at the top of the page without any title or rubric, and there is nothing to indicate the end but the spacing and the beginning of the immediately follow-ing piece near the middle of the page (f. 138): 'Incipit Epistola Alex-

---

[7] One of the tales, No. xxix, was printed by the present writer as a contribution to the study of 'The Wager Cycle, in *Mod. Lang. Notes*, vol. xxiv pp. 218-222 (Nov. 1909). This tale and two others constituting the last three tales of the Worc. Cath. Libr. collection, all of which are apparently spurious later additions to the original, were also printed, along with their Latin originals, by Hilka and Söderhjelm (*op. cit.*, I. Anhang II, pp. 68-73).

[8] This Ms. has often been described in recent years, so that it will not be neces-sary to repeat the description here. Cf. Hulme, 'A Valuable Middle English Manu-script.' *Mod. Philol.* vol. iv, p. 67 ff. (July, 1906); Floyer and Hamilton, *A Catalogue of Manuscripts Preserved in the Chapter Library of Worcester*, Oxford, 1906; Hulme, *The Harrowing of Hell*, etc., EETS (extra Ser.) 100, London, 1907, 'Introduction, p. xlviii ff.; Hulme, *Richard Rolle of Hampole's Mending of Life*, from, etc., *Western Reserve Studies*, vol. I, no. 4, 'Introduction,' pp. 5-11.

andri Magni Regis Macedonum ad Magistrum suum Aristotilem'. There are forty lines to a page and the writing tho' rather small is easy to read.

The Worcester version omits eight of the tales found in the complete Mss. of the original Latin *Disciplina* (cf. Hilka & Söderhjelm *op. cit.*), but as noted above, there are three tales added at the end.[9]

The Middle English translation was carelessly made; there are numerous instances in which the translator seems to have been in a hurry, or ignorant of the Latin text he was following. Many of these crudities are pointed out in the footnotes of this edition. The stories, moreover, do not always follow the order they occupied in the original, and occasionally a passage has been taken out of its natural setting and connection in the Latin version by the translator (or perhaps by the copyist of the Worc. Cath. Ms.) and shifted to a different part of the collection. Indeed, the confusion about the meaning of the Latin and the arrangement of the materials often suggest the probability that we have to do with a careless copy of an earlier original. One might, to be sure, discover that many of these peculiarities have their basis in the Cambr. Univ. Libr. Ms. (li, vi, ii, ff. 95-116) of the Latin version, which, as we have already seen, is the source of the final three tales of our collection. Hilka and Söderhjelm, however, have not recorded many notable textual differences between this and the other complete manuscript versions— except the three spurious tales—either in their introductory discussions[10] or their foot notes.

---

[9] The missing tales are Nos. VII, VIII (cf. I, 13), XII (I, 16, l. 9), XVIII (I, 20), XXI (I, 29), XXIX (I, 41), XXXI, XXXII (I, 43-44); the additions (Nos. XXVIII-XXX) seem to have corresponding originals in only one of the Latin Mss., viz. Cambridge Univ. Libr. li, 6, 11, ff., 113a-114 (see Hilka & Söderhjelm *op. cit.* I, Anhang II.) The identification of this Ms. and the definite determination of its relation to the Worc. Cath. Libr.' Ms. F. 172, is only one of the many merits of this excellent edition of the Latin *Disciplina Clericalis*.

[10] Cf. *op. cit.* I, pp. xi, xvi, xix—where the editors remark: "C¹ has the noteworthy assertion (I, i) that Petrus was the physician of Henry I, king of England" . . . . and "the copyist was in general fond of making additions." They also observe that the interpolation of the three spurious tales just after the closing words of the piece caused the shifting of exempla xx, xxii, xxiv from their natural positions in the collection to the end of this version—also pp. 68 and 72.

PETER ALPHONSE'S DISCIPLINA CLERICALIS

A COMPLETE MIDDLE ENGLISH VERSION
FROM
THE WORCESTER CATHEDRAL LIBRARY MS. F. 172.
PROLOG[11] (f. 118b)

Petir Alfons seruaunt of Jhesu Crist, maker of this booke saith:
Thankynges I do to god the whiche is first and without bigynnyng, to
whom is the bigynnyng and the end and of all goodenes the
fulfillyng Sapiens and wisdam; whiche sapiens and reason whiche
aspirith vs with his wisdam, and of his wounderful reason with
cliernes shyneth and with manyfold maner of the holigost with his
grace vs hath enriched. Forwhi therfor god though I beyng a
synner vouchestsauf to cloth me with many maner wisdams, ne
that the lantern to me taken be nat hid vnder a busshel; but with
stiryng of the same spirite to the profite of many to make and com-
powne this booke I am monysshed and warned, beseechyng hym
as to the bigynnyng of this my litel booke he enjoyne a goode end;
me also kepe that nothyng in it be saide that to his wil be displeasure.
Amen[12]

The paragraph omitted from the Introduction (see I, 1-2) by
the English translator runs as follows: May God then who con-
strained me to write this little book and to translate it into Latin
aid me in the undertaking. For when I wished to know by my own
efforts the source of human life, I discovered that intellect was given
to man by God for this purpose, that he might be zealous in the
study of sacred philosophy as long as he lives; for by this he will
gain more and better knowledge about his Creator and will strive to
live temperately and know how to protect himself against threaten-
ing misfortunes; and he may thus follow that path in the world that
leads to the kingdom of heaven. And if he lives according to these
precepts of sacred discipline, he will fulfill the purpose for which
he was created and will deserve to be called perfect. Moreover, I
have considered that man's nature is weak, so that he must be
assisted and instructed in a few things if he is not to fall into a state

---

[11] The prolog indicated in Ms. only by paragraphing.

[12] The long paragraph immediately following in the Latin is omitted in the English.
There is in fact evidence everywhere that this translator (or possibly the copyist of this
Ms.) was both ignorant of the Latin and careless. He pays no attention to prolog or
epilog; he frequently omits words, clauses, sentences, and sometimes extensive passages
from the original; he occasionally transfers a passage from its natural connection in
the Latin; and the instances of his misunderstanding and mistranslating the Latin are
almost countless.
  I shall attempt to supply free translations, for the sake of the connection in the
narrative, of all omissions of any length and importance. Wherever there is any
doubt as to the meaning of a word or passage the original Latin will also be given in the
footnotes.

of utter weariness. He must also preserve his strength of mind, so that he may more easily remember the means by which his nature is to be softened and sweetened. For if this is forgotten he will require many other things to make him recall what he has forgotten.

I have therefore composed this little book partly from the sayings and warnings of philosophers, partly from Arabic proverbs and admonitions both in prose and verse, and partly from fables about animals and birds. And I have carefully considered the method, so that, should I write at great length, the contents might not be a hindrance instead of a help to the reader; but that both reader and hearer might have an opportunity and a desire to commit them to memory. And they who gain knowledge by means of this book will recall the things they have forgotten. The title of the book is one growing out of its theme, that is, *Clericalis Disciplina;* for it treats of the trained priest. But I have decided to exclude everything, as far as possible, from this treatise that is contrary to our belief or different from our faith. To this end may the omnipotent God on whom I rely assist me. Amen.

If to any man this litel Epistil renne bi his vtter eye and sumwhat in it he shal see that kyndely cause and nature to his more subtil eye,[13] eft and eft I monysshe and do warne he ageyn to Rede.[14] And last to hym and to al thoe that bien of parfite feith of holichirche I sette and put to correccioun. Forwhi and forsoth the Philosophre trowith nat any thyng to be parfite in mannes invenciouns or fyndynges.

Therfor Enoch the philosophre, whiche in Arabik tung is named Edriche, saide to his sone: "The dreede of god be thy busynes and lucre and wynnyng shal come to the without any labour." Another Philosophre saith: "Who that dredith the lord al thynges dreeden hym. Forsoth who that dredith nat god is adred of al thyng." Another philosophre saith: "Who that loveth god dredith god. And who that lovith god is obedient vnto god."[15]

Socrates saide to his disciples: "See ye that ye bien nat seide obedient and inobedient in the same." The Enucheies[16] saiden vnto hym: "What seistow to vs leve Ipocresy?" [He said]: "Forsoth it is Ipocresy for to make symulacioun of obedience to god bifore men and in hid thyng or secret to be in-

---

[13] Lat. I, 2, l. 12, quod humana parum cavit natura viderit, subtiliori oculo.

[14] Lat. iterum et iterum relegere moneo.

[15] The English version omits the saying of the next speaker in the Latin, 1, 2, 1. 22. The Arab said in his verse: "It is incredible that thou art disobedient to God and yet pretendest to love him; if thou truly lovedst him thou wouldst obey him. For he that loves obeys."

[16] or Emicheies; the translator did not know the Latin form Enuclea, imper. sing. from enucleo—are, 'to explain,' and consequently gave a false interpretation of this sentence, Enuclea nobis quod dicis, meaning "explain or make clear to us what you are saying"

obedient."[17] On of his disciples saide vnto hym: "Ther is non other people but of Ipocrisy, therfor to a mannes soule it is goode to beware."[18] Socrates saith: "Ther is sum man whiche prevy and apert shevith hymsilf to be obedient vnto god, as that he be had holy among men and therfor of theym the more to be worshipped. Ther is another more subtile whiche levith and forsakith this Ipocresy, as that he may (f. 119) deserve to the more. Forsoth whan he fastith or any almesse doeth, and of hym be asked if he hath do, he aunswerith: 'God knowith or nat,' as in more reverence he be nat had; and it is saide non Ipocresy the whiche wil nat shewe his goode deede vnto men.[19] Also I bileve and I trowe that ther bien but fewe whiche bien percyuers[20] in this maner of Ipocresy. See yee therfor that this ne deprive yow nat the Rewarde of yowre labour, that it fal ne hap nat, al thynges that ye don with cleen intencioun ye seeke nat therof to have any glorie." Another Philosophre saith: "If thow bihold stidefastly into god, althynges shuln be prosperous to the wherever thow goest."

Balaam whiche in Arabik tung is cald Lucan saide to his sone: "Sone, ne is nat the ampt, otherwise cald pismer, wiser than thou, whiche gadrith in somer wherof he livith in wynter? Sone, ne is nat the Cok more waccheful than thow, whiche in the morow wakith and thow sleepist? Sone, ne is nat the Cok strenger than thow, whiche iustifieth x wifes and thow maist nat chastise oon? Sone, ne is nat the dog or the hound more nobil than thow, whiche of his benefactours is remembred and myndefull and thow of thy bene-factours art foryeetful? Sone, ne be it seen to the a litel to have oon enemy, or to moche to have a thowsand friendis. Forsoth I say to the forwhi."

I. THE HALF FRIEND.

Whan Arabs shude die [he] cald his sone vnto hym and saide: "Sey thow while I live how many friendes thow hast purchaced." The sone aunswerd and saide: "I arbitre and trust that I have pur-chaced mo than a hundred[21] friendis." Than the fader saide: "The

---

[17] Lat. I, 2, l. 25. Dicunt ei: Enuclea nobis quod dicis. Qui ait: Dimittite ypocrisim! Est enim ypocrisis, et cet.

[18] Lat. Estne aliud genus ypocrisis, unde homini cavendum sit?

[19] The Latin for this confusing sentence runs (I, 3, l. 2): Cum enim ieiunat vel elemosinam facit et ab eo quaeritur si fecerit, respondet: Deus scit! vel: non, ut in maiori reverentia habeatur et dicatur quia ypocrita non est qui hominibus factum suum nolit propalari.

[20] This reading is doubtful; Lat. Credo etiam paucos esse qui aliquo huius ypocrisis genere non participent.

[21] Ms. C.

philosophre saith, 'Ne praise thow nat a friend til thow have proved hym.' I sith the tyme that I was born and have lived vnneth I have purchased half a friend. Thow therfor how hastow purchaced a hundred?[21] Goo therfor to proeve hem all, as thow maist know if any be thy parfite friende." The sone said: "How counseilest thow that I shal proeve hem?" [The fader said]: "Sle a Calf and breke hym smal and put hym in a sack, so as the sack be infect with bloode withoutfurth, and than [go] to thi friende; sai thow; 'Dere friend, I have slayn a man; I pray the to burye hym secretely, so as noman shal have the suspect and so maistow save me'." The sone dide as his fader bad hym. Forsoth the first that he came to saide vnto hym: 'Bere the ded man with the vpon thi neck; so as thow hast don evil, so suffre thow satisfaccioun. Forsoth he shal nat entre in to myn house.' And when he had don so bi all, thei aunswerden the same. Therfor goyng ageyn to his fader [he] told hym what he (f. 119b) had don. Than the fader saide: "It happith to the as the philosophre saide to his sone. 'Many friendis bien nombred in prosperitee but a fewe in necessite.' Go to myn half friend that I have and see what he saith to the." He com and as he had saide to other he saide to this. The whiche saide: "Entre in to myn house; this is no seker place to be shewed vnto neighburghs." Therfor he sent out of his house his wif and al his houshold and digged a pitte. Whan he saw al thynges redy and arraied al thynges as it ought to be, he departed doyng thankynges, and therof rehersed vnto his fader what he had do. Forsoth the fader saide, "For suche oon the Philosophre saith: 'he is a veray triewe friend that helpith the whan al the world failith'." Then saide the sone to the fader: "Hastow seen any man whiche hath wonne or purchaced hym suche an holl friend?" [The fader answerd]: "I have nat seen that, but I have herd [it]." Than the sone: "Tel me of hym if happely I myght purchace me suche a friend." Than quod the fader:

II. THE TWO PERFECT FRIENDS.

"Relacioun[22] and told it is to me of ii busy merchauntis, the whiche that oon dwellid in Egipt and that other at Baldach, so only bi heryngsay thei knewen toguyder and bi messangiers bitwene senten for their necessaijs. It happened that[23] he of Baldach went of his neede and busynes into Egipt. The Egipcian heryng of his comyng mette hym and with grete joye toke hym in to his house and

[22] Lat. I, 4, l. 11. At pater : Relatum est mihi.
[23] 'That' repeated in Ms.

in al thynges served hym as is the maner of friendis bi viii daies, and shewid hym al his manoirs and other juels and necessaries[24] to hym bilongyng whiche that he had in his house. At the viii daies end he of Baldach sekeled.[25] That gretely greved the lord of the hous, [whiche] cald vnto hym al the lechis of egipt, as they come to his house to see his friende. The lechis felt his puls eft and eft, also bihield his vryne, and non infirmyte in hym thei knew. Therfor thei knewen [it] to be a passioun of love. This knowen, the lord of the house asked hym and bisought hym if ther were any womman in his hous that he loved. To that the sikeman saide: 'Shewe me al the wymmen of thyn house, if that haply amonges theym I may see hir that I love, and I shal tel the.' Whiche so herd, [he] shewid hym syngeressis and dauncers, of the whiche non of hem hym pleased. After that he shewed al his owne doughters; thiese also as tho other he refused and non Reward of hem tooke. The lord forsoth of the house had a nobil damysel and maiden whiche long[26] tyme he had norisshid and cherissed to that entent with hymsilf to have maried (f. 120). Whiche whan he had shewid hym, the sike man forsoth bihied and saide: 'Of this and in this is my lif and deth.' Whiche whan the lord of the house herd [he] yaf to hym that noble faire maide vnto wif with al tho thynges whiche was with hyr to bi taken, vp suche condicioun that he shuld wed hir vnto wif. These thynges complete, [he] toke his wif and tho thynges whiche he tok with his wif, and his neede and busynes don repaired ageyn home in to his cuntrey.

Forsoth it happed after that this Egipcien in many maners lost al his goodis and was made a veray needy poore man [and] thought in hymsilf that he shuld go to his friend whiche he had at Baldach, as that he myght have mercy and pite vpon hym. Therfor naked and hungry in the tempest and silence of the nyght he cam to Baldach. Shame forsoth so withstoode hym that he went nat to the house of his friende lest haply unknowen at suche tyme he were forbode the house. Therfor he entrid in suche a temple where he benyghted. But in lase while than he wold ther abide[27] [he] mette ther two men of the Citee nyhs to the temple, of whiche that oon slowgh that other and p[r]ivily fled. Many of the Citizeyns for the

---

[24] Lat. (I, 4, 1. 15) has simply: ostendit ei omnes manerias cantus quas habebat in domo sua.

[25] For this sentence the Lat. has Finitis octo diebus infirmatus est.

[26] Two or three letters crossed out in Ms.

[27] Translator has rendered Latin entirely wrong (I, 5, 1. 9), Sed cum ibi anxius multa secum diu volveret.

noise and the cry ran and founde a man slayn and sought what he
myght be that did the manslaughter, entred the temple hopyng to
fynde the mansleer ther. Fyndyng ther the Egipcian and askyng
of hym wherfor he had slayn the man, he heryng this of theym[28]
saide: 'I am he that hath slayn the man; coveityng deth so to end
his pover[te]'. And so was he taken and imprisoned, and on the
morow brought bifore the juges and to the deth condempned and to
the gibet and for to execucioun. Many forsoth ther were in that
maner that met hym, of the whiche oon was his friende of whos
cause[29] he cam [to] Baldach, and sharply beholdyng hym tooke hym
to be his friend whiche he left in Egipt. Remembryng also of the
goodenes whiche he had done to hym in Egipt, thynkyng forwhi that
after his deth he myght nat yield nor acquite hym his goode deede,
decreed in hymsilf for hym to die. And with a grete voice cryeng,
'What condempne yee an innocent? Whider wiln yee leede [hym]
that no deth hath deserved? It is I that hath the man slayn.' Than
thei laiden handis on hym and hym bond and hym led with that
other toward the gybet for to have execucioun; and that other from
the peyne of deth loosed and absoiled. The mansleer beyng in the
same pres, biholdyng and seeyng this, than went with theym and
saide in hymsilf[30]; 'I have slayn the man (f. 120b) and this is
dampned. And here another innocent is deputed vnto turment, and I
forsoth that hath don the nuysaunce goeth free. What is the cause
of this maner of justice I wote nat, but that only it be of the grete
suffraunce and pacience of god. Forsoth I knowe that god is a
veray just juge and no hid synne levith vnpunysshed. And lest that
he herafter take on me more harder vengeaunce, so of this maner of
blame I shal nat deferre me to be gilty. And so from deth I shal
assoile and loose [hym] to purge and clense the synne that I have
don.' [He] obeied hymsilf[31] therfor to the perel saieng: 'I, I whiche
hath don the evil; thiese that ye han dampned[32], leve yee hem
vnhurt.' Forsoth the juges nat a litel woundryng thiese[33] other from
deth delyvered they bond. And now nat a litel[34] of jugement
doubtyng this with thiese other bifore delyvred ledden bifore the
kyng and to hym al told and rehersed bi order and hym also com-

---

[28] Lat. (I. 5, l. 13) audierunt ab ipso quia ego illum interfeci.
[29] Ms. 'cauj'; Lat. cuius causa.
[30] These three words inserted on margin.
[31] Lat. (I, 6, l. 1) obiecit se ergo periculo dicens.
[32] 'that ...... dampned' not in the Latin, which has istum dimittite in noxium.
[33] Lat. (I, 6, l. 2) hunc.
[34] The preceding three words supplied on margin.

pellid to doute. So bi a comune counsail they goyng[35] to hem, al the cryme and blame that to theym was put, he pardond on covenaunt that they shulden shewe the causes of the cryme and blame to hem put. And they forsoth bi comune assent told hym the trowth of the thyng and of al wern assoiled[36]. The denzyn[37] whiche had decreed to die for his friende led hym in to his house [and] of al the worship to hym bifore don saide: 'If thow wilt rest quietely and dwel with me, al thinges as it bihovith shuln be to vs comune. If forsoth thow wilt go ageyn[38], al thynges whiche that I have and be myn, evenly we shuln departe.' Than he softly and swetely thanked hym of his yudenes, submytted hym to that he hym offred in particioun received, and so went hom ageyn in to his cuntrey[39]." Thiese thinges reherced and told, saide the sone to the fader: "Vnneth may any man fynde suche a friend."[40] Another philosopher said about untried friends: "Provide thyself once with enemies and a thousand times with friends, for thy friend may perhaps become an enemy sometime, and it will thus be easier to bear thy loss." Another philosopher also: "Avoid seeking counsel of any one until he has proved faithful to thee." Another philosopher again: "Give thy friend as much good advice as thou canst, even though he will not believe thee; for it is just that thou give him good advice, although the silly man may not follow it." Another: "Do not reveal thy counsel to every man; for it is better to seek counsel of him who retains it in his heart." Suche a phil[os]opher saith:[41] "Thyn hid and secrete counsail as is in thi prison shit, forsoth opened and shewed, holdith the as bounden in his prisoun."[42] Another: "Never associate with enemies when thou canst find other companions; for they will notice when thou doest evil, but fail to see the good things thou doest."

A certain poet said: "It is one of the serious misfortunes of this world that a free man must sometimes accept the help of his enemy. A man once inquired of a certain Arab: 'What is the worst misfortune that can happen to thee in this world?' The Arab: 'When necessity compels me to ask my enemy to give me what I wish'." Another: "Do not associate with a lecher for his society is a disgrace to thee." Another: "Do not exult in the praise of a lecher, for his praise is blame and his blame praise for thee." As a certain

---

[35] 'y' and 'go' are wanting because the left corner of the leaf has been torn off and pasted on again.

[36] Lat. (I, 6, l. 6) Communi autem consensu omnibus absolutis.

[37] Lat. indigena.

[38] Lat. (I, 6, l. 9) Si vero repatriare volueris.

[39] Lat. has for last sentence only sicque repatriavit.

[40] At this point the translator has omitted several sentences of the long dialogue (I, 6, l. 12-9) connecting exampla II and III.

[41] Lat. I, 6, l. 22, Alius.

[42] This sentence is followed by a further omission of the sayings of several philosophers from the Latin, see I, 6, l. 24 ff.

philosopher was passing along the highway he found another philosopher jesting with a lecher and said to him: "Birds of feather flock together." But that one replied: "I did not associate myself with him." To this the wayfarer: "Then why dost thou approve of him?" And he: "I do not, but in great need even an honest man must resort to a privy." Another philosopher: "Son, it is difficult to climb high houses but easy to descend from them." Another philosopher saide to his sone: "Bettir is the enymite of a wiseman than the friendship of a foole." Another saith: "Ne have thow nat for no grete thyng the frendship of a foole, forwhi it is nat to the abidyng." Another: "Bettir is the felawship of a simple man nurisshed among sapient men than led and brought furth with feders of prudent men."[43] Another: "Swetter it is to a wise man sharp lif amonge wise men than swete lif among vnwise men." Another saith: "Ther bien two maners and spices of wisdam: that oon is na (f. 121) tural and that other artificial, of the whiche that oon may nat be without that other." [Another]: "Ne committe thow nat wisdam vnto foolis, forwhi vnto theym it is but an iniury; neither denye thow it nat vnto wise men, for that that is theirs thow takest awey from hem."[44] Another: "The gifts of this world are of different kinds; for some are given riches, some wisdom. A certain man speaking to his son said: "Which wouldest thou prefer to have given thee, money or wisdom?" To this the son: "That which others are most in need of. There was once a certain wise poet who, though distinguished, was poor and in need, and who was always complaining about his poverty to his friends, about which also he composed verses expressing some such sentiment as this: 'Thou who rejoicest in wealth, show me why I am in want. Thou art not to blame, but tell me, who is to blame? For if my lot is hard, it surely was not made so by thee. But thou art mediator and judge between me and my destiny. Thou hast given me wisdom without wealth; tell me then, what can wisdom do without wealth? Take thou a part of my wisdom and give me some of thy wealth. Do not make me suffer such want that its hardships will bring disgrace upon me'."[45] A certain philosopher said: "Everyone appears to another in one of three different relations: To whomsoever thou doest a kindness thou seemest to him to be greater than himself; from whomsoever thou desirest nothing thou seemest to be on an equality with him; but to whomsoever thou art indebted for any favor thou seemest to him less than himself." Another: "Wisdom is the light of the soul, but sense is the light of the body." Another:

---

[43] Lat. (I, 7, 1. 15) quam prudentis cum leccatoribus educati.
[44] After this speech the Middle English version again leaves out several sentences of the Latin.
[45] See I, 8, 1. 3.

"Wisdom revives even dead bodies by its light, as the rain by its moisture revives the dry earth."

The disciple saide to the Maister: "How shal I behave me to be accompted among sapient disciples?" The Maister: "Kepe scilence til it be necessary and neede to the to speke." Another Philosopher: "Only Silence is a wisdam and to speke[46] is a signe of foly." [Another]: "Ne hast thow nat to aunswer til an end be of the asker[47]; nor any questioun made in felawship ne tempt thow nat to assoile while thow biholdist ther any wiser than thow; neither answer thow nat to any question made to anothe[r]; neither have thow appetite of lawde or praisyng for thyng to the vnknowen. [For the philosopher says]: 'Who of thyng to hym vnknowen appetith lawde or praisyng yieldith to prove hymsilf a lier'," Another: "Be thow restful, stil, and quiete vnto trowth, whether it be saide of the or obiect agenst the." [Another]: "Ne have thow no glory in thi wise wordis, for as the Philosopher witnessith, 'Who that glorieth in wise wordis provith hymsilf to be a foole.' Doyng thow al thiese thynges thov shalt be even nombred among disciples of sapience and of prudence."

[The philosopher says]: "Who can prudently inquire prudently vndirstandith the solucioun." [Another]: "Whosumever shameth to folowe the wisdam of other, more he shameth the same of hym to be inquired." Another: "Who that for a short tyme shameth to suffre loore, al tyme in shame and vnwisdam shal dwel and abide." [Another]: "Nat all tho whiche is saide sapient is sapient; but he that lierneth wisdam and can reteyne it." Another: "Who that in doctryne faileth, litel his kynred or gentilnes profiteth or availith. Nobilnes needith loore, sapience forsoth and experience." Another: "In whom the nobilnes of elders failith or endith or covenably reservith."[48] Another: "Nobility that proceeds from my own exertions is more precious to me than that which comes to me from my father."

.   III.   The King and the Poets.[49]

Arabs: "Suche a versifiour prudent and curteys but vnnoble of byrth to a kyng offred his vers; whos prudence noted the kyng hym with worship tooke. Therfor to this other versifiers envieden to

---

[46] Lat. (I, 8, l. 10) loquacitas est, et cet.

[47] Lat. finis interrogationis.

[48] Lat. (I, 8, l. 27) Alius: In quo sua desinit nobilitas, avorum nobilitatem haut congrue reservat. The speech of the next philosopher was omitted by the translator.

[49] I, 9, I, 1.

overcome his gentilnes and kynred, gadreden toguyder and saiden vnto the kyng: "Sir kyng, whi this so vile of birth magnifieth [thow] somoche?" To this the kyng: "Whom yee han trowed to blame, the more yee han praised." He forsoth whiche was blamed to this he adjoyned: "Roses spryngen on thornes nat for that[50] they bien nat (f. 121ᵇ) blasfemed." Forsoth the kyng left hym with more worshipful giftes.

It happened as that a versifiour of noble birth forsoth but litel lierned to suche a kyng offred his vers. Whiche the kyng tooke, as gretely evil made, dispised hem, and nought yave hym. Therfor the versifiour saide to the kyng: "If nat only for the vers, for myn nobilnes sumwhat yield thow me." Therfor the kyng: "Who is thy fader?" Than he shewed hym. Than quod the kyng: "Seede in the hath he gendred."[51] To whom the versifiour: "Often of whete spryngith Rye." To this the kyng saide: "Thow previst thisilf lasse than thi fader." And so [he] left hym vnrewarded.

Another versifiour also cam to the kyng of an vnnoble fader but a gentil Moder. What compownd and vncompownd he offred hym vers whos moder had a shyneng brother. Forsoth nat forthan toke [he] hym worshipfully, [but], asked of hym whos sone he was.[52] Than he pretendid hym his vncle; wherof the kyng turned hymsilf in to moche laughter. Than saide his housold meyne: "Wherof procedith this laughter?" Quod the kyng: "Suche a fable in suche a booke I Red whiche I behold here with myn eyen." Quod thei: "What is that?" Quod the kyng.

IV. THE MULE AND THE FOX.[53]

"A Mule newly born fonde foxes in lesewes and woundryng saide vnto hym: 'Who artow?' The Mule saide hym to be formed.[54] To whom the foxes: 'Hastow neither fader ne moder?' [The mule replied]: 'A gentil hors is myn vncle.' So as [the mule] therfor knowlached nat the Asse his fader, insomoche that he was a slow beest and dul, so this shameth to knowlache his fader for his dulnes nat vnknowen." The kyng only turned hym to the versi-

---

[50] Ms. 'than.'

[51] Lat. Semen in te degeneravit (I, 9, 1. 10).

[52] For the passage 'What compownd .... sone he was' the Lat. has (I, 9, 1. 13) Incompositus quidem incompositos obtulit versus. Cuius mater fratrem habebat et facetia splendidum. Rex autem nequaquam eum honorifice suscepit. Quaesivit tamen ab eo cuius filius erat.

[53] I, 9, 1. 18.

[54] These words only partially translate the Latin, mulus dicit se Dei creaturam esse.

fiour and saide: "I wil that thow shewe me thi fader." And he shewed [hym]. Therfor the kyng knew that his fader was vnlierned and saide to his seruauntis: "Departe this from our thynges, forwhy he hath goten ne deservid hem."[55]

The Arab said to his father: "It astonishes me to read that in past ages nobles, wits and wise men were honored, but only lechers were revered." To this the father; "Son, be not astonished that priests honor priests, nobles nobles, wits wits, and that lechers are venerated by lechers." The son: "And I read another thing: that priests were not honored for their wisdom; whence lechers were produced and came to great honor." Then the father said to him: "That indeed resulted from the indolence of the time." To this the son: "Explain to me, dearest father, the true meaning of nobility." And the father: "As Aristotle says in his letter to King Alexander,[56] in reply to the question as to what kind of a man he should select for his counsellor: 'Choose a man,' he said, 'who has been educated in the seven liberal arts, disciplined in the seven cardinal virtues, and polished by means of the seven accomplishments, and I believe he will represent perfect nobility'." And the son: "Such nobility does not exist today, for all the nobility that I know about proceeds from gold and silver. As the poet says: 'Riches exalt people who are without nobility and poverty degrades an ancient house that was once in high esteem because of its nobility.' A certain poet made these verses about the evils of the world which are destroying its nobles. 'Tell them,' he said, 'who despise us because of the misfortunes which befall us, that this world shows its opposition to no one but the noble. Dost thou not see how the ocean carries dung and chaff away, but how precious stones go to the bottom? And dost thou not see that the stars in the heavens are without number, and yet none of them but the sun and moon are subject to eclipses'?" And the father: "This happens on account of the indolence of the world, since men decide that riches are the sole reason for boasting." One of the disciples questioning the master said: "Since there are seven arts, seven accomplishments, and seven virtues, I wish you would tell me what they are." The master: "All right; these are the seven arts: Logic, arithmetic, geometry, physics, music, astronomy. Opinions vary greatly as to what the seventh is: philosophers who believe in prognostications assert that necromancy is the seventh. Others who do not believe in predictions think philosophy is the seventh, which excels the study of nature and the elements of the earth. Some who do not know philosophy insist that it is grammar.

Then, the accomplishments are: Riding, swimming, archery, boxing, the chase, chess, writing verse. The virtues (industriae) are:

---

[55] After this sentence the M. E. version has omitted a long passage of the philosophical discussions of the original (I, 9, 1. 26). The first half of the passage discusses "true nobility"; the second half, "the seven arts, virtues, and crafts."

[56] A Middle English version of this letter is preserved in the same Ms. (ff. 138-148) with the *Disciplina Clericalis*.

not to be a glutton, a drunkard, a sybarite, not to be given to violence, to lying, covetous, and of evil life." The disciple: "At the present time I do not believe there is any man of this kind." After this long omission the Middle English version resumes the narrative.

Suche a Philosophre correctid his sone sayeng: "Beware of lesynges, for it is swetter than flessh of briddis." Quod another: "How light it is to bryng furth a lesyng; whi is trowth seen so hard and hevy?" [Another philosopher]: "If thow dredist trewth wherof forthynkith he, bettir it is ever to say so."[57] [Another]: "Shame it is to deny lest it brynge to the necessite of lesyng; forsoth more honest it is to denye a thyng than[58] to yeve long terme." Another: "To blame of blames to adde to the preyer is this tyme with warenes to deny."[59] Another philosopher: "If lesyng savith any, moche more with trowth he shalbe saved." Suche on accused was led and brought bifore the kyng, the juge denyeng the cryme to hym put and of the same convicte. To whom the kyng: "In duble wise thow shalt be punysshed (f. 122), oones for the cryme don, the secunde for the deede denyed." Another suche in likewise accused that he had don, nat denyed. Thei that stooden aboute saiden to the kyng, he to take jugement of the deede.[60] "Nat so," quod the kyng, "forwhi the philosopher saith: 'To hym that confessith the synne, reason it is to Reles the jugement.' So he departed from the kyng free."

Socrates saith: "So as a manlyer[61] is nat convenient in the felawship of a prince, so is he excluded from the kyngdom of hevenes". Forwhi the philosopher saide to his sone: "Say thow hym a lier whiche to overcom evil saith evil; forwhi as fier hurtith nat fier, so evil vnto evil ne fallith nat. Therfor as water quenchith fier, so goode thynges distroieth every evil." [Another]: "Ne yield thow nat evil, ne be thow nat like vnto evil. So yield thow goode as that thow be the better vnto evil."[62]

The Arabik saide to his sone: "If thov see oon bifore greved of evil werkis, ne entremete; who loosith the[63] doute, vpon hym shal the thretenynges be."

___

[57] Lat. (I, 11, l. 6.) Si dicere metuas unde paeniteas, melius est dicere: non! quam sic!

[58] Ms. 'that.'

[59] Lat. (I, 11, l. 9.) Terminum termino addere roganti est hoc tempore calliditas negandi.

[60] Lat. (I, 11, l. 13)Dixeruntque qui regi astiterunt: Decrimine confesso iudicium sumet.

[61] Lat. homo mendax.

[62] The M. E. omits the immediately following sentence, Alius: Ne confidas in malo si periculum evaseris, ut aliud ineas, quia illud non faciet u simile pertranseas (see I, 11, l. 22).

[63] Lat. quia qui pendulum solverit.

V. THE UNGRATEFUL SERPENT.[64]

"Suche oon passyng bi the woode fonde a serpent of shepardis strayned and to stokkes bounden, whom in maner loosed cured to chaufe.[65] The serpent chauffed aboute the faverer bigan to gnawe and bite and somoche the bond hard he constreyned. Than the man saide: 'What doestow? Whi yieldistow evil for goode?' The serpent saide: 'I do my nature and kynde.' Quod he: 'And I have don wele to the, and that evil doestow only to me?' So they strivyng wern cald to the jugement of the fox. To whom whan he was com [and] was shewed al the matier bi order, than the fox saide: 'This cause can I nat deme bi heryng, but as it was at the first bitwixt yow I may see it at eye.' Than was the serpent bounde ageyn as she was afore. 'Now,' quod the fox, 'thow serpent, if thow maist eschape, departe.' Whiche to the man: 'To loose the serpent nil thow nat labour.' Whether hastow nat Red, 'who that loosith the dowte, vpon hym shalbe the falle'."[66]

The Arabik saide to his sone: "If thow be[67] any tyme and maist lightly be delyvered, abide nat to long; for while thow abidest haply ther may falle a more grevous blame, as fil to the gibbous or courbed of the versifiour." "And how," quod the sone? [The fader]:

VI. THE POET TURNED PORTER.[68]

"Suche a versifiour [was] makyng vers to a kyng, and the kyng praised his wisdam [and] bad hym aske a yift for his deede. The whiche asked suche a thyng as for to be a porter at oon of the yates of the Citee bi the space of a Moneth, and to have of every courbed man a peny[69] and of every ooneyed a peny, of every scald a peny, of every lepre a peny, of every Roughhered a peny (f. 122[b]). Whiche that the Kyng graunted and strengthed with his seale; whiche in his mynisterie taken and in his seruice and office sat at the yaate. In a day suche a courbed and wele hooded [man] beryng a staf in his hand wold han entred. To whom the versifiour mette askyng hym a peny, whiche he denyed. And with strength the versifiour pullid of his hoode and tooke with oon eye, and asked of two pens, where that first he myght have escaped with oo peny;

---

64 I, 12, l. 1.
65 Lat. Quem mox solutum calefacere curavit.
66 Lat. ruina erit.
67 Lat. gravatus fueris.
68 I, 12, l. 13.
69 M. E. version omits et a scabioso denarium.

but [he] withhield it and nat havyng any help wold have fled. But
he hield hym bi the hoode and pullid of his Cappe, and than his
hede appiered scalled, for the whiche than he asked thre pens. Than
this courbed man seeyng hymsilf havyng non help nor myght nat
flee bigan to Resiste and withstond with naked armes, in whiche
[he] apperid [a] lepre; for the whiche than he asked the fourth
peny. To whom the defendaunt tooke awey his capp and cast it
to the grounde, and [he] appered than Roughered, for the whiche
than he toke of hym five pens. So it happed for that he wold [nat]
paie oo peny, vnwares paied fyve pens.[70]" A certain philosopher
said to his son: "Son, refrain from passing through the house of
wicked people, for passing results in stopping, and stopping leads
to sitting and sitting ends in a deed. It is related, by way of illus-
tration, that two priests went forth from the city one evening for
a walk, and they came to a house where some drinkers had met
together.

A Priest in the House of Drinkers[71]

Petrus Alphonsus tellis how on a tyme two clerkis went
samen before a place ther thar was many drynkers, and thai
callid thaim in. And the tone of thaim went into thaim and the
toder wold nott, bod went on hys wais; and it was fer within
nyght. So the wachis of the town fande all thies drynkers syttand
samen, and the clerk with thaim, and becauce a man of the town
was robbid that nyght, thai tuke thaim all and the clerk with thaim,
and hanged thaim. And the clerke at bade with thaim, or he was
hanged, sayd on this maner of wyse; "Quisquis inique gentis con-
sorcio fruitur, procul dubio mortis immerite penas lucratur. What-
somevur he be at vsis ill company, na dowte of he sall hafe ane
ill dead.[72]"

The Latin version of this tale (No. vii, see I, 12, l. 2) is as
follows: Dictum enim est duos clericos de ciuitate quadam vespere
ut exspatiarentur exisse. Venerunt ergo in locum ubi potatores
convenerant. Dixit alter socio suo: Divertamus alia via, quia philosophus dicit: Non est transeundum per sedem gentis iniquae.
Respondit socius: Transitus non novebit, si aliud non affuerit. Et
transeuntes andierunt in domo catilenam. Substitit alter retentus

---

[70] At this point two short exampla are omitted from our English version; these
occur in the Latin (I, 13) as Nos. VII and VIII and have the titles, *About a Priest enter-
ing the House of Drinkers* (*Exemplum de Clerico domum potatorum intrante*) and *The
Voice of the Owl* (*Exemplum de voce bubonis*). The English also omits the brief discussion which links VI and VII together in the Latin (I, 12, l. 28).

[71] This exemplum in an abbreviated form is found in the Middle English *Alphabet
of Tales* (Ed. Banks, Pt. II, No. 721, p. 483).

[72] I have preserved the spelling and punctuation of the EETS edition, only substi-
tuting *th* for the early English *thorn* and *and* for &.

dulcedine cantus. Monuit socius ire: noluit. Recedente socio remansit solus illectusque cantu domum intravit. Undique vocatus sedit sedensque cum aliis potavit. Et ecce preco exploratorem civitatis fugientem sequens post illum domum protantium intravit. Invento exploratore in illa domo ipse et omnes capti sunt. Hic, inquit, hospitium huius exploratoris fuit: hinc exiit, huc rediit; omnes conscii et socii huius fuistis. Ducti sunt omnes ad patibulum, et clericus inter illos magna voce praedicabat omnibus: Quisquis iniquae gentis consortio fruitur, procul dubio mortis immeritae poenas lucratur.

The Voice of the Owl.[73]

"It is reported of two disciples that in going out of a certain city they came to a place where the voice of a woman was heard very distinctly, and the words of the song were well written and the music of the song was so arranged that it sounded beautifully and delightfully.. One of them stopped on account of the beauty of the song, but his companion said to him: 'Let's turn aside'. And they did it; for one is so far deceived by the song of a bird that he may be led to death. Then the one said: 'This voice is sweeter than that which my master and I heard long ago'. 'What kind of voice was that', asked the other, 'and how did you hear it?' 'It happened,' the companion said, 'that we had gone out of the city and we heard a very harsh voice in an unattractive song, and the words sounded discordantly; the one who sang repeated the words frequently and lingered over the unmelodious song as if it was delightful.' Then the master said to me: 'If it is true as men say, that the voice of the owl portends the death of some one, then that is without doubt the voice of an owl fortelling death.' To this I said: 'I wonder, if the song is so dreadful, why this man alone is delighted with it?' And he answered me: 'Dost not thou remember the philosopher who says: "Man takes delight in three things even though they may not be good: in his own voice, his own song, and his own son"?' After he told this about himself and his master they both went away."

A certain philosopher said to his son: "Follow a scorpion, a lion, and a dragon, but do not follow a wicked woman." Another philosopher said: "Pray God that he keep thee from the snares of vile women, and be thyself on guard lest thou be deceived. For it is said about a certain philosopher that in passing by the place where a fowler had stretched a net for snaring birds, he saw a base woman in wanton sport with the fowler and said to him: 'While thou art trying to snare birds, be careful that thou art not caught in the filth of the lime thou preparedst for he birds'."[74]

---

[73] I, 13, 1. 12 ff.

[74] Here the English version takes up the thread of the narrative again, reproducing a lengthy paragraph of the Latin (I, 14, ll. 1-12) as sort of connecting links between tales VI, VII, VIII and IX of the original.

Suche a disciple saide to his Maister: "I have Rad in wordis of Philosophres whiche comaunden a man to kepe hym from the froward wit and engyne of wymmen. And [Salomon] only in the same proverbes amonestith and warneth. If thow therfor any thing above the wiles of hem memoratief holdist I wold with tellyng thow woldist teche and lierne me, outher of fables outher of proverbis." [The Maister]: "That cause shal I do to the gladly. But I am ashamed lest any simple soule redyng oure ditees whiche of the craftis of wymmen to the correccioun of theym and thyn and to instruccioun and liernyng of other seen. That is for to say how, nat knowyng ne wityng their husbondis, [they] callen and clepen their loves and with hem abiden, clippyng and kissyng; and so of theym and in theym accomplisshen and fulfillen their lascivic and foul lustis, trowyng the wikkidnes and cursidnes to Rebounde in vs."[75] The disciple than saide: "Maister, ne dreede nat that forwhi Salamon in the booke of proverbis and many sapient men whiche to correcte suche evil and shrewd maners of theym wrote suche thynges therof they deserved no blame, but laude and praisyng. And thow in like wise writyng theym to our profite[76] shalt deserve no blame but a corowne of glorie; and of this praier or tellyng shewe thow." Than the Maister:

VII.[77]   THE VINE-DRESSER DECEIVED BY HIS WIFE.

"Suche a man went to cut his vyne. That his wif seeyng than[78] vndirstode hym to dwelle and tarie long aboute it and sent a messangier to cal (f. 123) hir love and lemman, and arraied a feeste. Forsoth it happened and fil so that the lord of the vyne smyten with a braunche in the eye, yeede ageyn anon vnto his house nothyng seeyng with the hurt eye. Comyng to the gate of his [house he] knocked at the doore. That the wif withynfurth [heryng] gretly troubled cald hir love and hid hym, and after that opened the doore vnto hir husbonde. Whiche entryng and gretly sorrowyng for his hurt eye bad array his chamber and make his bedde, as that he myght rest hym. The wif dred lest he entryng the chamber shuld see hir love ther hid, and saide: 'What hastest thow to bedde? First tel me what is the befalle.' And he told hir what was hym befalle. 'O diere sir,' quod she, 'soeffre me that I conferme with

---

[75] This is a crude translation of the original of I, 14, 11. 4-8.
[76] Lat. (I, 14, 1. 11) de illis scribens ad nostram utilitatem....sed coronam promereberis.
[77] This is No. IV in the Latin, I, 14, 1. 13.
[78] Ms. 'that'.

craft of medicyne and charme that it come nat to the hool eye as is comen to the hurt eye, forwhi thi hurt and damage is comune to vs both,' settyng hir mowth to the hol eye til hir love from the place wher he was hid went his wey and departed, vnwityng the husbond. Than quod she: 'Arise now, diere husbond, for I am sure it shall nat come to the holl eye that is come to the hurt. Now maistow, if it please the to go to thy bedde.' And so was the husbond scorned and bijaped of his wif."[79]

Then the disciple said to his master: "Thou hast advised me well, and what thou hast told me about their guile and wiles I commend to the thirsty and yearning soul; and I would not exchange what I have learned about it for the riches of the Arabs. But if thou pleasest to proceed, instruct me how we may succeed in converting it into action for the future direction of the public." "I will do it," said the master.

VIII[80] THE HUSBAND DECEIVED BY MEANS OF A SHEET.

"It is saide that suche oon went on pilgremage and committed his wif vnto his stepmoder.[81] Whiche wif loved another and shewed it vnto hir moder, whiche even moeved for hir doughter yaf a favour to the lover and cald hym and bigan to talke[82] apart with hym and with the doughter to feede and to feeste. And in their feestyng came the husbond to the dore and knocked. And the wif arisyng hid the lover and after that opened the doore, whiche after he was entred [he] bad array his bedde for he wold rest hym, insomoche that he was wery. The wif was troubled and in doubte what she shuld do. The Moder seeyng that saide vnto the doughter: 'Ne haastow nat to arraie his bedde til we han shewed to thy husbond the lynnen that we han made.' And thold wif drewe out the lynnen as moche as she mgyht to a corner and toke hir doughter another end to another corner. Whiche lynnen [was] so stretched and lift vp in height. And so was the husbond mocked and bijaped til the lovier that was hid went out at the doore. Than saide thold wif vnto hir doughter: 'Stretche this lynnen vpon thi husbondes bedde, forwhi myn handis and thyn han made (f. 123b) it and woven it.' To whom the husbond saide: 'And thow, lady or dame, canstow array suche lynnen?' 'O sone, moche have I made and

---

[79] There is nothing in the Latin (cf. I, 14, 1. 26) corresponding to this sentence. And the following discussion which connects exempla IX and X in the Latin version is omitted from the English.

[80] No. X in the original, I, 15, 1. 1.

[81] Ms. 'vnto his wif vnto his stepmoder' (Lat. socrui, 'mother-in-law.')

[82] Ms. 'take.'

arraied in this maner.' In this maner is the husbond disceived of his wif."[88]

To this the disciple: "What I have heard is wonderful; but I wish thou wouldest give me more advice, for the more I consider the nature of those women the more I am concerned about my own protection." The master replied: "To this end I will tell you a third tale and then our exempla will suffice for thy instruction." The disciple: "If it please thee."

IX.[84] THE MOTHER-IN-LAW WITH THE DRAWN SWORD.

It is also had in relacioun that suche a pilgrym commytted his wif to his stepmoder to kepe. The wif secretly loved a yong man; that to hir moder redily she told and shewed. She forsoth consentyng to the lover arraied a feeste and cald hym therto; whiche so feestyng the husbond cam and knocked at the gate. The wif therfor aros and lete the husbond [enter]. But the Moder with the doughters love remayneng, forwhy ther was no place wher to huyde hym, doubted what she and he shuld do. But while the doughter opened the dore vnto hir husbond thold wif tooke a naked swerd and yaf to the lover [and] bad hym to stonde streight bifore thentre of hir doughters husbond with the same swerd drawen. 'And if the husbond saye ought vnto the, aunswer nat ageyn.' And he dide as he was boden. The dore opened [and] the husbond seeyng hym standyng so askid hym what he was; the whiche aunswerd nat. Than if he were abasshed at the first sight, in that he yaf non aunswer, he drad moche more. . Than thold wif aunswerd: 'Dere sone, be stille lest any man here the.' To that he wondryng saide: 'What is that, faire dame?' Than thold wif: 'Thre yong men pursued this man hider and we than opened the dore [and] suffred hym to entre thus with his swerd til thei wern gon that wold have slayne hym. Whiche now dredith the to be oon of theym, is astonyed and aunswerith nat.' Than the husbond saide: 'Wele mote ye fare that in this maner han delyvered hym from deth.' And so entryng [he] cald his wifes love and made hym to sitte with hym. And so with swete spechis sported hem and at nyght leete hym go."[85]

---

[88] For this sentence see Latin I, 15, l. 12 f.

[84] No. XI in the original, I, 15, l. 16 ff.

[85] The Worcester version omits the tale which follows this immediately in the Latin, (No. XXII) *The King and his Jester or Storyteller* (cf. I, 16, l. 9); but since the tale in a slightly different version was printed by Caxton in 1483 (see Introduction p. 9), I supply this *lacuna* by reprinting it from Caxton's first edition. There it is No. 8, 'The eyght fable is of the discyple and of the sheep.'

The King and His Jester

A discyple was somtyme whiche toke his playsyre to reherce and telle many fables, the whiche prayd to his mayster that he wold reherce vnto hym a long fable. To whome the mayster ansuerd: "Kepe and beware wel that hit happe not to vs as it happed to a kynge and to his fabulatour." And the discyple ansuerd: "My mayster, I pray the to telle to me how it befelle." And thenne the mayster sayd to his discyple:[86] "Somtyme was a kynge whiche hadde a fabulatour, the whiche reherced to hym at euery tyme that he wold sleep fyue fables for to reioysshe the kynge and for to make hym falle in to a slepe. It bifelle thenne on a daye that the kynge was moche sorowful and so heuy that he coude in no wyse falle a slepe. And after that the sayd fabulator had told and reherced (f. 128b) his fyue fables the kynge desyred to here more. And thenne the sayd fabulatour recyted vnto hym thre fables wel shorte. And the kynge thenne sayd to hym: 'I wold fayne here one wel longe, and thenne shalle I leue wel the slepe.' The fabulatour thenne reherced vnto hym suche a fable: Of a ryche man whiche wente to the market or feyre for to bye sheep; the whiche man bought a thowsand sheep. And as he was retornynge fro the feyre, he cam vnto a ryuer, and bycause of the grete wawes[87] of the water he coude nat passe ouer the brydge. Neuertheles he went soo longe to and fro on the ryuage of the sayd ryuer, that at the last he fonde a narowe way[88] vpon the whiche myght passe scant ynough thre sheep attones. And thus he passed and had them ouer one after another. And hyderto reherced of this fable[89] the fabulatour felle on slepe. And anon after the kynge awoke the fabulatour and sayd to hym in this manere: 'I pray the that thow wylt make an ende of thy fable.' And the fabulatour ansuerd to hym in this manere: 'Syre, this ryuer is ryght grete and the ship is lytyll,[90] wherfore late the marzhaunt doo passe ouer his sheep; and after I shalle make an ende of my fable.' And thenne was the kynge wel appeased and pacyfyed.

And therfore be thow (f. 129) content of that I have reherced vnto the. For there is folke so[91] superstycious or capaxe that they may not be contented with fewe wordes."[92]

The disciple said: "It is recorded in ancient proverbs that he who grieves because of his possessions does not suffer as severely as he who is afflicted with pains of his body. And the story teller did not love his king as much as thou lovest me, for he only wished to divert the king's mind a little with stories, which was not thy inten-

---

[86] Jacobs reads 'descyple.'
[87] Jacobs reads 'waiues.'
[88] Lat. (I, 16, 1. 19) exiguam naviculam.
[89] Lat. His dictis fabulator obdormivit.
[90] Jacobs 'lytyl.'
[91] Jacobs omits 'so.'
[92] There is no punctuation in Caxton's text except vertical lines at the ends of sentences. I have also normalized the capitalization, otherwise no changes are made. Caxton's last two sentences—which are in reality a translation of Steinhöwel—are quite different from the Latin (cf. I, 16, 1. 26): Quodsi amplius me praedictis etiam subtexere alia compuleris, iam dicti praesidio exempli me deliberare conabor. And there is nothing in Caxton which corresponds to the latter part of the connecting dialogue between Nos. XII and XIII of the Latin version.

tion with me at all. I pray thee, therefore, instruct me further, if
thou wilt, concerning the resourcefulness of women." The master
replied:

X.[93] THE PROCURESS AND HER WEEPING BITCH.

"It is saide that suche oon had a wif of a noble kynred, inly faire,
beautevous, and chast. So haply it fil that [he] with busynes of
Reason wold go to Rome. But he wold nat make non other depute
keper of his wif but hirsilf, he trusted so moche in hir chast maners
and of worshipful proef. Forsoth this man redy went furth with
felawship. The wif forsoth lived chastly and in al thynges prudently
doyng remayned. So it fil that of necessite compulsed out of hir
owne house [she] went out to hir neyghburgh in felawship. That
neede and busynes don [she] went hir hom to hir owne house. That
suche a yong man bihielde and with brennyng love bigan to love hir
and many messangiers (f. 124) sent vnto hir coveityng of hir whom
he so brennyngly loved; Eft[94] to whom with contemptis [she] hym
vttirly dispised. The yongman whan he felt hymsilf so dispised,
was made so moche sorowyng and over moche kynde of sikenes
hevied and greved. Oftentymes here and ther wher he sigh that
faire womman goyng out desiryng with hir to meete and felawship, but in no wise it myght availe. To whom for sorowe weepyng he mette with an old wif clenly clad in Religious habite askyng
of hym what was the cause that compelled hym so to sorowe. But
the yongman so avexed and troubled in his conscience wold nat
discovere. To whom thold wif saide: 'How moche that a sike man
hidith and takith awey the knowlache of his infirmyte from his
leche, so moche more grevous and sharp shal his grevaunce and sikenes be.' Whiche so heryng [he] told hir bi order and shewid hir
al his secrete counsail of this that hym bifil. To whom thold
wif: 'Of this whiche now thow hast saide with goddis help I shal
fynde a Remedie.' And so left hym and went hir hom to hir
house. And a litel whelp that she had at hom [she] made it to fast
two daies without mete; and the thrid day to the fastyng hound
yaf brede jnowogh with an oynoun[95] froted. Whiche whan the
hound had tasted and eten for the bitternes the eyen bigan to teare.
After this that old wif went hir to the house of the shamefast
womman whom the yongman loved so moche; whiche worshipfully

[93] No. XIII in the original, I, 17, l. 3.
[94] The Ms. reading appears to be 'Of' or 'Ef to:' the Lat. (I, 17, l. 10) has this simple sentence: Quibus contemptis eum penitus sprevit.
[95] Lat. sinapi i. e. 'mustard'.

for the gretnes of hir Religioun with a demure spirite toke hir in. To this forsoth folowed hir whelp. Whan this goode womman saw that litel hound so weepyng [she] askid what it had and ailed . and wherfor it so the eyen tered and wept. To this thold wif aunswerd: 'Diere friende, ne aske nat what is the cause forwhi it is so grete a sorow that I may nat tel it.' Forsoth the womman somoche the [more] stired hir to telle. Than thold wif or old Vek saide: 'This litel hounde the whiche thow biholdist was my doughter, a chast maiden and a faire and right beautevous, whom suche a yongman loved; but she was so chast that in althyng vttirly his love she dispised.[96] Wherof he somoche sorowyng was streyned in to a grete sikenes; for the whiche blame wrecchidly my doughter here is chaunged in to an hounde.' And this saide, for grete sorowe she brake out in teeris wepyng, that old wif. To that the goode womman: 'What! therfor diere dame, I feele mysilf that I am made in like synne. Me forsoth a yongman lovith, but of my chastite his love I have vttirly dispised, and in like maner to hym it fallith.' To whom that old wif: 'Ewer I praise the, my diere friende, but rather (f. 124[b]) than this wrecchidnes of eschaunge in to an hounde shuld fal to the, do that he askith and desirith. If forsoth I had knowen the love bytwene the forsaide yongman and my doughter, mi doughter shuld never have be[n] chaunged.' To whom the chast womman saide: 'I beseche the as in this thyng that thow tel me holsum and profitable counsail that my forme and shap be nat deprived and made like an hound.' To whom thold wif: 'For the love of god[97] right gladly, and forwhi of the, my doughter, I am merciful and have on the compassioun; and that forsaide yongman I shal seeke if he may be'in any place founde and bryng hym vnto' the.' To whom the womman dide thankynges. And so thold wif with hir crafty spechis and wordis yaf hir feith; and the yongman whom she promysed brought and so felawshipped hem toguyder."

"A," quod the disciple to the Maister, "Never herd I of suche a mervaile, whiche as I trowe was don bi craft of the devil." Quod the Maister: "Ne doubte the nat it was so." Than quod the disciple: "I hope if any suche man were so sapient, as alwey he drad hym how he myght be disceived bi the engyne and craft of womman haply he myght kepe hym from hir engyne and wiles." Quod the Maister: "I have herde of suche a man whiche that moche laboured,

---

[96] Lat. ut eum omnino sperneret et eius amorem respueret. See I, 17, 1. 27.
[97] Lat. Pro Dei amore et animae remedio meae.

as in kepyng of his wif, but nothyng it profited hym." The disciple saide: "Goode Maister, tel me what he dide that I may knowe if I wed that womman how I may kepe hir." [The maister]:

XI.[98] THE JEALOUS HUSBAND AND THE STONE CAST INTO THE WELL

"Svche a yong man ther was whiche al his entent and al his wit and yit moreover al his body[99] set and put to knowe al the maner and craft of wymmen, and this don nold no wif wedde.[100] But first [he] went to seeke counsail and cam to a man most sapient of that Regioun and asked and sought how he myght kepe his wif if he wold any wedde. The sapient man forsoth heryng this · yave hym counsail that he shuld make an house with high wallis of stone and put his wif withyn and yeve hir mete inowgh to ete and no superfluite of clothyng; so that in that house be but oo dore and oo wyndowe bi whiche she may see, and of suche height and of suche composicioun and makyng bi whiche noman may entre ne go out. The yongman forsoth heryng this counsail of the sapient man dide as he bad hym. Forsoth erly in the morow whan the yongman went out, [he] shit the doore of the house fast, and in like wise whan he entred; and whan he slept hid the keyes vnder his hede and thus dide long tyme. Suche (f. 125) a day while this yongman went out his wif as she was wont ascended vp to the wyndow [101] and while she stoode ther she sawe another faire yongman of body and of face, with whiche sight anon she was kyndeled in the love of hym. Forsoth the womman so kyndeled in the love of that yongman and as it is above saide in suche warde and straite kepyng bigan to thynk how and bi what art or craft she myght speke with that yongman. And she ful of engyne and guyle craftily bithought hir to stele the keyes of hir lord hir husbond while that he slept, and so she dide. Forsoth hir lord hir husbond was in custom every nyght to be drunk of wyne; now the more suerly myght she go out to hir love and fulfil hir volunte and lust. The lord forsoth, of that Philosophres techyng and warnyng withouten guyle of any act of womman, bigan to thynke what his wif often and daily wold with drynkyng make hym drunke. Suche

---

[98] XIV in the original (I, 18, 1. 18).

[99] Lat. (I, 18, 1. 18) totam intentionem suam et totum sensum suum et adhuc totum tempus suum.

[100] This last sentence conveys the opposite meaning to that of the Latin, I, 18, 1. 19, et hoc facto voluit ducere uxorem.

[101] Eng. version omits et euntes et regredientes intente aspexit. I, 19, 1. 2.

a tyme was that she trowed hir husband drunke ;[102] of whiche the
womman [ignorant][103] aros out of hir bedde in the nyght and went
to the doore of the house and opened and went hir out to hir love.
Hir husbond in the scilence and stilnes of the nyght softly arisyng
cam to the doore and founde it open and shit it and made it fast and
went vp to the wyndowe and stoode ther in his shirte[104] til that
he sawe his wif torne ageyn willyng to entre and founde the doore
shit. Wherof hir soule sorowed and so [she] knokked at the
doore. The husbond heryng his wif and seeyng and as he knewe
nat asked what she was; and she askyng foryevenes promyttyng
never to do more so. In this it profited hir nat, but the husbond
in his wrath saide that she shuld nat be suffred ther to entre, but
to his friendes[105] and hirs it shuld be shewed. But she the more
and more cryeng saide that but if he opened the doore she wold
skippe in to the pitte the whiche that was next the house and so
end hir lif; and so of hir deth he shuld yield reason to hir friendis
and neighburghs. He dispisyng his wifes threatis and manacis wold
nat suffre hir to entre. The womman ful of art and guyle toke vp
a grete ston and cast in the diche, to this entent that hir husbond
heryng the sowne of the stoon fallyng in to the diche shuld trowe
that she were falle into the diche; and this don she hid hir secretely
bihynde the diche. The simple man and vnwise heryng a maner
sowne of fallyng in to the diche without and tarieng went out
of his hous in a grete haasty cours wenyng and trowyng
that his wif had lept in to the diche. But the womman
seyng the dore open, nat foryeteful of hir craft entred the house
and shit the (f. 125ᵇ) dore fast and went vp to the wyndow. He
seeyng hymsilf so disceived saide: 'O thow false guyleful and ful
of the devils craft, suffre me to entre and whatsumever thow hast
don to me, wihoutfurth bileeve thow for a soth that I foryeve it.'
To whom with grete blamyng and vttirly with othis sweryng [she]
saide he shuld no entre have ther. And moreover saide: 'O thow
traitor, of thi cursid deedis I shall shewe vnto [thy parents] forwhi
every nyght thow art wont thiefly to go from me and go to thi
strumpettis.' And so she dide. The friendis forsoth heryng this
estemed and trowed it for a sooth and blamed the man. And so
was the womman delyvered with hir fals craft, and al the wite and

---

[102] Lat. (I, 19, l. 10) Quod ut sub oculo poneret, se finxit ebrium esse.

[103] Lat. Cuius rei mulier inscia.

[104] Lat. (I, 19, l. 13) stetitque ibi donec in camisia sua mulierem suam nudam revertentem vidit.

[105] Lat. suum suis parentibus.

peyne that she deserved torned vnto the man; to whom it profited nat anymore his wif to kepe. Forwhi also an hepe of wrecchidnes fil vnto this man, for the most dele of the people bilieveden that he hadde deserved this that he suffred."[100] Than quod the disciple: "Ther nys no man whiche may kepe hym from thengyne and wilis of womman but if that god kepe hym. So bi this tale I shal nat wedde bicause of this exhortacioun."[107] Than quod the Maister: "This oughtist thow [nat] to bileeve of al wymmen, forwhi grete chastite and[108] grete goodenes is Repared and arraied in many wymmen, and wite thow that in a goode womman may be arrettid goode felawship. A goode womman also is a feithful keper and a goode house. Salamon in thend of his proverbis made xxii verse of the laude and the goodenes of wymmen." To this the disciple saide: "Wele hastow comforted me. But herdistow ever of any suche womman whiche that torned hir wit and hir engyne vnto goode?" Quod the Maister: "I have herd." Quod the disciple: "Tel me of hir, for that were to me novelte and grete wounder." The Maister:

XII.[109] THE TALE OF THE TEN COFFERS.

"It is saide to me that suche a man of Spayne went to Miche and while he went he cam in to Egipt; whiche wold entre and pas thurgh the deserte [and] thought to leve his money in Egipt. And bifore that he would leve it he asked if any feithful man were in that Regioun to whom he myght leve it. And an auncient man shewed hym to a man named of goodenes and of trewth, to whom he left a thowsand talentis. From that he went furth and made anend of his journey and cam ageyn to hym to whom he committed his money, and this that he to hym commytted asked. But he ful of wikkednesse saide that he never had seen hym tofore. Forsoth he so disceived went to the goode men of that Regioun and told to hem and reherced how he to whom he had commytted his money hadde hym entreatid. Forsoth neighburghs heryng suche thynges of (f. 126) hym wolden nat bileeve it, but saiden it myght nat be but that he had lost his money. So every day he went to the house of hym to whom he commytted his money[110] [and] with

[106] The last sentence of the tale in the Latin was omitted by the English translator (I, 20, l. 10), Wherefore at the compulsion of most good people, deprived of his dignities, lowered in esteem on account of slander from his wife, he had to suffer the penalty of incest.

[107] Lat. (I, 20, l. 14) est magna dehortatio.

[108] Ms. 'at.'

[109] No. XV in the original, I, 20, l. 22.

[110] Lat. (I, 21, l. 4) illius qui retinebat iniuste pecuniam.

faire wordis and speche besought hym to yielde hym his money.
Whiche that the disceivour herying blamed hym and saide that if
he any more cam or spak therof he shuld suffre grevous peyne as
he was worthy. He heryng the threatis and manacis of hym that
disceived hym went his wey and bigan to sorowe; and in his goyng
ageyne met with anold womman clad in heremytal clothyng,—
this freal and fieble old wif supportyng hirsilf with hir staf, re-
moevyng the stones out of their place, [and] praisyng god that no
passyngby hurt nat their feete at hem. The whiche seeyng the man
wepyng, knewe hym for a straunger [and] moeved with pitee cald
hym in to help [hym] and what was hym bifalle asked hym. And
he bi order told. Forsoth the womman heryng the wordis of the
man saide: 'Friend, if the wordis bien triewe that thow hast saide,
I shal do the help.' And he: 'In what maner, goode womman and
and goddis seruaunt?' Quod she than and saide: 'Bryng me a man
of thi lond and cuntrey to whom thow maist trust in word and
deede.' Than said he: 'I shal bryng [hym].' And sofurth to the
felaw of hym that was disceived comaunded x cofres preciously to
be peynted with dyvers colours withoutfurth, wele locked and
bounden with irn and silver, and filled ful of smale stones. and
bryng hem[111] vnto the house of his host. And he so dide. The
womman whan she sawe al thing arraied and redy as she bad, 'Now,'
quod she, 'seeke x men the whiche shuln go with me to the house
of hym that hath deceived the, and with thi felaw beryng the cofres
oon after another afer comyng. And as soone as the first is comen
in to the house[112] and hath rested, com thow and aske thi money,
and somoche I trust in god that thi money shalbe to the Restored.'
And he, as the old womman bad hym, he dide; whiche nat foryeteful
[when] taken to the house of the disceivour, with the felaw of the
disceived cam and saide:[113] 'Suche a man of Spayne [whiche] was
hosted with me and wold go to Mehe asked and sought bifore the
money whiche he hath in x cofres, to what goode man he myght
saufly commende it to kepe til he come ageyne. Also I beseche the
as of my cause in thi warde thow kepe, and forwhi I have herd
and also knowe the a goode man to be feithful and triewe, I wil
nonother but only the this money to be commendid vnto.' And
while they spaken thus cam he beryng the first cofre[114] so as he was

---

[111] Ms. 'the' or 'ye.'

[112] Lat. (I. 21, 1. 18 illius hominis qui te decepit.

[113] The Latin (I, 21, 1. 22) has, Quae non oblita incepti quod praedixerat iter
incepit. Et venit cum socio decepti ad domum deceptoris et inquit.

[114] The Lat. (I, 22, 1. 1) is different here, venit primus deferens cofrum, aliis a longe
iam apparentibus.

comaunded, and another after afer so a longe appieryng; the disceived [man] nat foryeteful of the old wommans comaundementis, cam after (f. 126ᵇ) the first cofre. Forsoth he whiche had hid the money, ful of wikkidnes and cursed craft, as he saw the man comyng to whom he had hid and denyed the money, dredyng lest he wold aske or enquire questions[115] of hem that dide do bryng thiese cofres of his money so taken and denyed, went agenst hym and saide: 'Friend, where hastow be and wher hast thow taried? Com and take thi money to me of trust commended, forwhi I have founde it and from hensfurth it werieth and lothith me to kepe it.' And than he glad and joyeng, Received the money doyng thankynges. Thold wif whan she sawe hym havyng his money, risyng saide: 'Go we both, I and my felawe, rennyng bifore agenst our cofres to haast hem; and thow forsoth abide til we come ageyn, and kepe wele that now we han brought.' He forsoth with a glad soule kept that he had take and abode the comyng of theym that myghten com after. And so with goode wit and engyne of thold wif the money was yolden."[116]

The disciple: "This was a remarkable and useful trick and I do not think any philosopher could think out a more subtle means by which man could recover his money more easily." The master: "A philosopher might well do by his natural and artificial skill and also by studying the secrets of nature what the woman did by her clever wits alone." The disciple: "I can well believe it; but if thou hast stored away in the treasury of thy heart anything of this character from the philosophers, pray bestow it on me, thy disciple, and I will commend it to faithful memory, so that I may at some time feed this most delicate morsel to those of my fellow disciples who have been brought up on the milk of philosophy. The master:

XIII.[117] The Ten Tuns of Oil.

"It happened that suche a man had a sone to whom after his deth nothyng he left sauf an house. This yong man with greate labour of his body lived and whiche with nature yeede vndir foote;[118] and though he were coarted and driven in grete nede, his house wold he nat selle. This chield had a neighburgh that was a grete Riche man whiche coveited to bie the house and yeve hym largely therfor. This chield forsoth wold nat selle it for price

---

[115] Lat. (I, 22, 1. 4) timens ne, si pecuniam requireret.
[116] The connecting link between this tale and the following one in the Latin (I, 22, 1. 13) was omitted by the translator.
[117] No. XVI in the original. See I, 22, 1. 20.
[118] Lat. Iste cum magno labore corpori suo vix etiam quae natura exigit suppeditabat.

ne for praier. After that the Richeman comprised with what engyne or what craft he myght thynke to betray this chield of his house. And this yong man after his power eschewed the faimiliarite of the Riche man. Therof the Richeman was sorowful bicause of the house that he myght nat disceive the chield, and vpon a day cam to the chield and saide: 'O goode [sir], leene me a litel part of thi court vpon a price, for in it vnder the erth x tonnes with oile wold I kepe, and nothyng shal it noye the and thow shalt have therof what sustenaunce of lif thow wilt.' The chield coarted with necessite[119] graunted and yave hym the keyes of the hous. Forsoth the yong man in the meane tyme of his fredam frely servyng askd his mete. And so the Richeman toke the keyes and the court of that yong man strangled and digged, and v Tonnes ful of oile ther laide and v half ful. And that don [he] cald the yongman and toke hym the keyes of the house and saide: 'O yongman, myn oyle to the I commytte and in to thi kepyng I betake.' The simple yongman trowyng al the tonnes ful in to his warde and kepyng received. And after long tyme it happened that (f. 127) in that lond oile was diere. The Richeman heryng[120] this saide to the chield, 'O my friende, com and help me to digge vp myn oile that to thy kepyng now I have comaunded,' and of his labour takyng a Reward. The yongman forsoth heryng his price and his praier graunted to the Richeman and after his power halp hym. The richeman nat foryeteful of his fraude and guyle brought men as to bie the oile. To whom whan he had brought [hem, he] opened the ground and v ful tonnes and v half tonnes ther thei founden. Perceivyng that, [he] cald the chield saieng thus vnto hym: 'Mi friende, bicause of thi kepyng I have lost myn oile; moreover that I commytted to the fraudelently thow hast taken awey; wherfor I wil that thow restore me.' This saide, wold he nold he hym to the justice he ladde, and whan he sawe the justice to hym he accused. But the yongman wist nat what he shuld say agenst it, but only askid triews and respite of a day. That the justice that was rightwis hym grauntid. Forsoth in that Citee ther dwellid such a philosophre whiche was named a grete helpdoer, a goode man, and a Religious. Forsoth the yongman heryng of his goodenes sent a messangier vnto hym and counsail of hym sought and asked saieng: 'If thei bien triewe that bien saide and told to me[121] of the, in homly maner do me help, for and for-

---

[119] Lat. (I, 23, 1. 3) coactus necessitate.
[120] Lat. videns.
[121] The English omits multis referentibus.

soth vniustly and wrongfully I am accused.' The philosopher herd the praier of the yongman [and] askid hym if he iustly or vniustly were accused. Forsoth he affermed with an oth vniustly. The philosophre heryng the thyng of trowth and moevid with pite saide that 'with goddis help I shal help the; but as of the Right thow hast taken respite vnto morow day, whiche tho thynges at thoo plees nil thow nat leve[122] and I shalbe redy to socoure thy trowth and to noisaunce of their falshed.' Forsoth the yonge man dide that the philosophre badde. Forsoth the morow after [he] cam to the philosopher to the Right; whom after the Right had seen as a [wise] man cald the philosophre, and so cald made hym to sitte next hym. Than the Right callid thaccusers and the accused and comaunded that thei shulden Reherse the plees; and so thei diden. Of theym forsoth standyng bifore, the Right saide to the philosophre that the causes of hem he shuld here and therof do iugement. Than the philosophre saide to the Right: 'Now comaunde yee that the cliere oile of the v ful tonnes be mesured and thow shalt knowe and wite how moche ther be of cliere oile; and in like wise of the v half tonnes and thow (f. 127[b]) shalt knowe how moche ther be of cliere oile. Than the thikke oyle of the v ful tonnes so measured and thow shalt know how moche thikke oile be in hem, and in like wise of the v half tonnes, if ther be asmoche as in the ful tonnes, know thow for a soth the oile is stolen. And if thow fynde in the half tonnes suche part of thikke oile as of cliere ther beyng went and issued out,[123] know thow for a sooth that oile nat to be stolen.' The Right heryng thus, confermed the iugement and so was don. And in this maner the yongman escaped with the wisdam of the philosophre. And so the plees endid, the yongman yielding thankynges to the philosophre. Than the philosopher saide vnto hym: 'Herdistow that never of the philosophre, "Ne bie thow non house bifore that thow knowe thi neighburgh".' To this the yong man: 'First we had an house that next vs hosted.' To whom the philosophre: 'First selle thyn hous bifore that thow dwel next a shrewde neighburgh'." The disciple: "Suche iugement appierith to be [of] the philosopher and this is the grace of god and meritorily is cald this name, the help of wrecchis."[124]

---

[122] Lat. (I, 23, l. 26) quin eas ad placita dimittere noli.

[123] The English omits, quod quidem et in plenis tonellis invenire poteris. See I, 24, l. 8.

[124] The short connecting link in the Latin is not given in the English. See I, 24, l. 15.

Then the disciple: "Though the things I have heard are fixed in my mind, yet they spur my soul on to wish to hear more." The Master said: "I will tell the gladly," and he began thus:

XIV.[125] THE TALE OF THE GOLDEN SERPENT

"It was saide of suche a Richeman in the Citee goyng, that a bagge ful with a thowsand talentis bare with hym and moreover a serpent of gold havyng eyen of jacynt in the same bagge, and al that he lost. And suche a poore man makyng ther his iourney fond it and yave it to his wif, and how that he found it to hir rehersed. The womman heryng this saide: 'That god hath yeven kepe we.' Another day a Bedil went bi the wey so to cry and to proclame: 'Who that hath founde suche money do yield it ageyn and without forfaiture or fraude he shall have therof an hundred talentis.' This heryng, the fynder of the money saide to his wif: 'Yield we the money and want any synne, we shuln have therof an hundred talentis.' To this the womman: 'If god had wold that he shuld enjoie the money he shuld nat have lost it. That god hath yeven kepe we.' The fynder of the money laboured as to yield it and she vttirly denyed it. And whether she wold or nold, to the lord he hath yold it and that he promised asked. ·The Richeman ful of wikkidnes saide: 'That me lackith another serpent wite yee.' This that he saide was [126] of a shrewde intencioun, as that he wold nat to the poore man yielde his promyse. The poore man saide he fonde nomore. And the men of that Citee fauorable to the Richeman, derogaunt and sharp agenst the fortune (f. 128) of poverte beryng hym haate, drewe hym and bitoke hym to the Right. Forsoth the poore man cried and swore, as it is above saide, that he fonde nomore. But while the word of this poore and richeman ran to the Ministres tellyng, the same smote and cam to the earis of the kyng. That as he had herd, called toguyder the Richeman and the poore and to hym[silf] comaunded to presente the money. Al thynges brought to the kyng, the philosophre whiche was cald the help of wrecchis with other sapient men cald and of his accusers to noye and to accuse, here and mark yee, the philosopher comaundith.[127] This herd [and] evenly moeved with pitee on the poore man, [he] cald hym vnto hym and saide: 'Tel me, my brother, if thow have the money of this man? that if thow have nat, with help

---

[125] No. XVII in the original (I, 24, 1. 18).

[126] Ms. 'this.'

[127] Lat. (I, 25, 1. 3) Adductis omnibus rex philosophum qui vocabatur Auxilium Miserorum cum aliis sapientibus ad se vocavit eisque· accusatoris vocem et accusati audire et enodare praecepit.

of god I shal deliver the.' To this the poore man saide: 'God
knowith that I have yielded as moche as I have founde.' Than the
philosopher vnto the kyng: 'If it please [the] to here, rightwis
iugement I shal say.' The kyng heryng this praied hym to deeme
and juge it.

Than the philosophre to the kyng: 'This[128] is moche more
credible and gretter witnesse of trowth hath, and it is nat to bileeve
nor trust hym that askith that he lost nat. And of that other partie
it seemyth to me Right credible that this goode poore man fond
nomore than he hath yolden, and forwhi if he were an evil or a fals
man, he wold nat have yolde that he hath yielded, but rather con-
celed and hid it.' Than the kyng: 'What forsoth demest thow,' quod
the kyng to the philosophre? The philosophre than to the kyng:
'Take the money and yeve therof vnto the poore man an hundred
talentis; and that remayneth kepe til he come that asked it, forwhi
this money is nat his; and this richeman went to the bedil and made
hym to aske the bagge with ii serpentis.' Forsoth it pleased to the
kyng this jugement and to al tho standyng aboute hym. Forsoth the
Richeman whiche had lost the bagge heryng this saide: 'Sir, and my
lord the kyng, in veray trowth I say to the the money was myn.
But forwhi that I wold take awey that the bedil promysed to this
poore man, yit hiderto I have saide I lacked another serpent. But
now my kyng, have mercy on me and that the bedil promysed I shal
yield to the pore man.' Than the kyng the money yieldid to the
Riche and the Richeman to the poore; and so with the wit and
engyne (f. 128ᵇ) of the philosopher the poore man was de-
livered."[129]

The link runs as follows in the Latin, beginning I, 25, l. 23:
The disciple: "This appears to be the spirit of philosophy, and
in the light of this exemplum Solomon's judgment concerning the
two women is not so remarkable."
The philosopher says: "Do not go on a journey with any man
unless you have known him previously. If any unknown person
joins thee on thy way and will learn about thy journey, tell him thou
wishest to go further than thou plannedst for; and if he carries a
lance go thou to the right; if a sword, go to the left."
The Arab corrected his son saying: "Follow beaten paths
though they are longer than bypaths." And again: "Take a maid
to wife though she be old." And again: "Bring thy wares to large
cities though thou expectest to sell them cheaper there." To this the

---

[128] Lat. (I, 25, l. 10) Iste homo dives bouns multum est et ut.
[129] After this tale the English version omits the immediately following link as well
as the succeeding tales of the Latin (No. XVIII) entitled The Path and The Ford (Lat.
a) Exemplum de semita (b) Exemplum de vado), cf. I, 26.

son: "What thou sayest about main roads is true.[130] For on a certain day when my companions and I wished to arrive in the city by sunset and were still a long way from it, we saw a footpath which it seemed would shorten the journey. But we met an old man and inquired of him about the course of that path. The old man said: 'The footpath leads more direct to the city than the highway and yet you will arrive there more quickly by the highway.' When we heard this we considered him a fool, and letting him proceed along the highway, we turned into the bypath. Pursuing this path now to the right and now to the left, we wandered about until it was night and did not reach the city. But if we had followed the main road we would no doubt have entered the walls of the city." The father replied to this:[131] "It happened to us differently as we were following the highway to the city; there was a river before us which we had to cross by some means before we could enter the city. And so, as we were proceeding on the journey we found the road divided, one fork of which led to the city through a ford, the other by a bridge. And then we saw an old man, of whom we inquired which of the two ways would bring us more quickly into the city. And the old man said the road by the ford was shorter by two miles than the road over the bridge. 'But, nevertheless,' he said, 'you will arrive in the city more quickly by the bridge,' And some of our party made fun of the old man, as certain of yours before did, and took the way across the ford. And some of them had their companions swept down by the current, others lost their horses and baggage, some had their clothes soaked with water, and others wept because their clothes were lost entirely. But we and our old man who crossed by the bridge proceeded without hindrance and any inconvenience and found them again, lamenting their losses on the bank of the river. To whom thus weeping and searching the depths of the river with rakes and nets the old man said: 'If you had gone with us across the bridge, you would not have had this delay.' But they replied: 'We did this because we did not wish to be delayed on the way.' And the old man answered to this: 'Now you are still more delayed.' Then we left them behind and joyfully entered the gates of the city. I once heard this proverb: 'The long road to heaven is preferable to the short road to hell'."

The fader saide to the sone:[132] "If thow be in the wey with any felaw, love thow hym as thisilf and thynk nat in any wise to disceive hym lest he disceive the, as ii Burgeis and a Cherl happed to felawship." Quod the sone: "Fader, tel me that as sum profite therof may be taken herafter." The fader saide:

---

[130] *Concerning a Footpath*, No. XVIII (a) I, 26.
[131] (b) *About a Ford* (I, 26, f. 14).
[132] Lat. (1, 27, 1. 1) Arabs castigavit filium suum.

XV.[133] THE THREE PILGRIMS TO MECCA AND THE LOAF

"It is saide of ii Burgeis and a Cherl [that] bicause of de-
vocioun went to Meche [and] that wern felawes at mete, whan[134]
thei comen nygh Meche theym failed vitaile, so that ther remayned
nothyng to theym but a litel meale or flour of the whiche they made
hem a litel lof. The burgeis forsoth seyng that saiden vnto hemsilf: 'We have but litel brede and our felaw is a grete eter, wherfor
it bihovith vs to have counsaile how we may withdrawe from hym
a part of [his] brede, and that vs ought to ete alonly ete we.' Than
thei token counsaile in this maner that thei shuld do make a cake
or a lof baken, and while it baked thei slept and everiche of the
Burgeis dreamed a woundirful swevene.[135] And or that thei leiden
hem to sleepe thei saiden to hemsilf: 'That while the cherl sleepith
craftily we shuln ete this brede that he shal nat wite ne knowe it.'[136]
And the cherl perceived the wikednes of the ii felawes, drewe the
brede out of the fuyre half baken and ete it and leide him doun.[137]
But oon of the burgeis so as he slept was agast and wooke and cald
to his felaw. To whom that other of the burgeis saide: 'How is
[it] with the?' Than he saide: 'I have seen a wounderful swevene.
Forwhi as it seemed to me that verily aungels[138] opened the yatis
of hevene and takyng me led me bifore god.' To whom his felaw:
'It is a mervailous swevene that thow hast seen. And I have
dreamed that ii angels ledyng me opened therth and brought me in
to helle.' The cherl heryng al this [was] feyneng hymsilf a sleepe.
But the disceived burgeys willyng [to] disceive hym callid the cherl
and awaked hym. The wily cherl as he had be agast aunswerd:
'What bien yee that callen me?' [Thei saide]: 'We bien thy
felawes.' And the cherl: 'Be yee now come ageyn?' Than they
ageyn to hym: 'Whider shuld we go from whens we ought to come?'
To this [the cherl]: 'It was seen to me in my visioun that forsoth
oon of yow was taken of aungels whiche[139] opened the yaatis of
hevene and led hym bifore god. And that that other was taken also
of aungels that opened therth and led hym doun to helle. I seeyng
thiese thynges [and] never trowyng of (f. 129) yowre comyng
ageyn, aros and eete vp the brede'." [And the fader]: "And so

---

[133] No. XIX in the original. See I, 27, l. 5.
[134] Ms. 'and whan'; Lat. douec venirent prope Mech.
[135] The English omits solus panem comederet.
[136] The preceding two sentences translate the Latin very freely: Hoc artificiose
dicebant, quia rusticum simplicem ad huiusmodi ficticia deputebant. Et fecerunt panem
miseruntque in ignem, deinde iacuerunt ut dormirent.
[137] The Latin has dormientibus sociis before the phrase 'out of the fuyre.'
[138] Lat. duo angeli.
[139] Ms. 'and.'

my sone, it happened and cam so to, that thei whiche wold han disceived their felaw that with his wit thei wern disceived."[140]

Then the son: "It happened to them as it is told in the proverb: 'He who wanted all lost all.' Such also is the nature of the dog whom they resemble: one of them tries to take away another's food. But if they followed the instinct of the camel they would imitate a gentler nature; for the nature of the camel is such, that when fodder is given to many of them at the same time, no one of them will eat until they can all eat together. And if one is so weak that he can not eat, the others refuse to eat until he is taken away. And since these peasants desired to assume the nature and manner of an animal, they should have followed the nature of the gentlest animal; and so they deserved to lose their food. But also I wish that could have happened to them which I have heard my master say happened once upon a time to the king's tailor instead of to his apprentice Nedwy, to wit, he was openly beaten with cudgels." The father replied to this: "Tell me, son, what you heard. What happened to the apprentice? for such a story will be a recreation to my soul." The son:

XVI.[141] THE MASTER TAILOR AND HIS APPRENTICE NEDWY

"It is saide[142] that suche a kyng had suche a Tailour the whiche dyvers tymes shoope to hym dyvers clothis apt vnto his body. And he had disciples and lerners of sowyng whiche everiche of hem craftily sowed.[143] Among the whiche [was] oo disciple named Nedwy whiche in the craft of [sowyng] was the best and past any of his felawes. But a grete feste day comyng the kyng cald vnto hym his tailour and his drapers and comaunded hem to array for the tyme comyng for hym and for his seruauntis precious clothis. That as soone and without any impedyment it were don, oon of his chambrelayns, a geldyng of whom was thoffice and the warde of sowers to kepe, addid and saide as that noon of hem observe ne kepe no croked nor long nailes, and praied that he shuld mynistre vnto hem sufficient necessaries. But in a day the mynistres of the kyng hote brede and hony with other disshes to the tailour and his felawship yaven to ete, and whiche that ther wern comaunded to ete. To whom so etyng saide the geldyng: 'Maister, whi ete yee, and Nedwy beyng absent neither yee abide hym nat?' Quod the Maister: 'Forwhi he etith no hony though he were here.' And so they eten. Than cam Nedwy and saide: 'Whi ete yee and I absent nor therof kepe my part?' Than

---

[140] The English omits most of the discussion between the father and son which serves as a connecting link between exampla XIX and XX of the Latin. See I, 28, l. 2 ff.

[141] No. XX in the original. See I, 28, l. 13.

[142] Lat. Narravit mihi magister meus.

[143] The English omits here quod magister incisor regis artificiose scindebat.

the geldyng saide: 'Thy Maister saide that thow etist no hony thowgh thow haddest bien here.' And he was stil and thought how that he myght recompense and quite his Maister. And this don Nedwy in his Maister absence secretly saide to the geldyng: 'Sir, my Maister is frentik and while he suffrith that he leesith his wit and vndiscretly betith and hurtith theym that bien aboute hym.' To whom the geldyng: 'If I knewe the tyme whan this to hym fallith, nat vnwarly don, I shuld bynde hym and with whippes correcte hym.' Than Nedwy saide: 'Whan thow seest hym bihold and looke hider and thider and betyng the grounde with his handis and risyng from his seete and castyng awey the stoole that he sat on with his hand, than thow maist knowe that he is out of his wit; and but if thow and thyne[144] provide with a staf he wil hurte or breke yowr (f. 129b) hedis.' To this the Geldyng: 'Blessid be thow; forwhi from hensfurth I shal purvey for me and myn.' Suche thynges saide, Nedwy the next suyng [day] secretly hid his Maister sheeris; and he[145] nat fyndyng hem bigan to smyte the grounde with his handis and to biholde here and there, arisyng from his seete and the stoole that he sat vpon to overterve. The geldyng seeyng this anon cald felawship and saide: 'Bynde yee the tailour that he ne bete ne smyte nonother and grevously bete ye hym.' But the tailour cried so and saide: 'What have I forfeted, or what or wherfor bete yee me thus?' But thei the more sharply betyn hym and wern stil forsoth. Whan they wern wery of betyng and scourgyng hym, thei leften and loosed hym only with the lif. The whiche respityng but a long while bitwene, asked of the geldyng what he had forfeted. To this the geldyng saide: 'Thi disciple Nedwy told me that whan thow art out of thi wit and woode that neither but in bondis and betynges thow be corrected, thow canst nat ceese; and therfor I bond the and bete the.' The tailour heryng this cald Nedwy his disciple and saide: 'Friend, whan knewistow me out of wit?' To this[146] the disciple: 'Whan knewistow me nat to ete hony?' The geldyng and other heryng this lawghed and demed ever either worthi his penaunce that he had taken.' To this the fader saide: "Meritorily this fil, forwhi if he had kept that Moyses comaunded as to love his brother as hymsilf, this had nat[147] happed or come vnto hym."[148]

The link contains the following: The wise man reproved his son saying: "Be careful to make no charges against thy companion

<hr>

[144] Lat. nisi tibi et tuis provideris; 'with a staf' not in Lat.
[145] English omits At incisor quaerens forfices. I, 29, l. 2.
[146] 'This' repeated in Ms.
[147] 'hadde nat' repeated in Ms.
[148] The rest of the link and the immediately following tale of the original version (*The Two Jesters—De doubus ioculatoribus*) are omitted in the English translation.

either seriously or in sport, lest it befall thee as it befell the two jesters before the king." To this the son: "Tell me about that father, I pray thee." The father: "All right. A certain jester once came to the king, whom the king made to sit at meat with another jester. But the latter began to be envious of the new comer after his arrival because the king had favored him more than himself and all those about the court. And in order that this state of things might not last long he planned to put him in disgrace so that he would have to run away. Therefore while the others were eating the first jester put the bones together and placed them before his companion; and when the meal was finished he showed the king the pile of bones, arranged for the disgrace of his companion, saying sharply: 'My companion has eaten the covering of all those bones.' And the king looked at him with an angry scowl.. But the accused said to the king: 'Master I did it because my nature, as is human, required me to eat the flesh and throw away the bones; and my companion did what his nature, apparently that of a dog, demanded, in eating both flesh and bones'."

The philosopher said: "Honor thyself as the lesser person and give him of thy substance, just as thou wishest that the greater honor thee and give thee of his substance." Another: "It is indeed base for a rich man to be avaricious, but it is beautiful for man of moderate means to be liberal."[149]

The disciple saide to the Maister: "Write thow to me the diffinicioun of the largesse, the Auarous, and the Prodogus; that is to say, the large or free man, the Covetous man, and the wastour."[150] [The fader]: "Whiche yevith to whom it is to yeve and withholdith and reteyneth to whom it is to withold, is[151] large; and [whiche] forbedith to whom it is forboden and to whom it is nat forboden [is] covetous.[152] And who that yevith to whom it is nat to yeve is a wastour."[153]

"Do not engage in a business that is failing, and do not delay to become associated with a growing business." Another: "A little happiness is of more worth than a house full of gold and silver." Another: "Strive for the useful with great care, not with great haste." Another: "Do not look upon one richer than thyself lest thou sin against him, but upon one who is poorer than thyself and then thank God." Another: "Do not deny God because of poverty, and do not be proud because of riches," Another: "He who desires much is always consumed with hunger for more." Another: "If you only wish to have as much in this world as will suffice for

---

[149] At this point in the connecting link between tales XXI and XXII of the Latin (cf. I, p. 30) the Middle English takes up the thread of the story again.

[150] Lat. (I, 30, l. 1) Discipulus ait: Diffinitionem largi et avari et prodigi mihi subscribe. Pater, et cet.

[151] Ms. 'and'.

[152] Ms. 'and covetous to whom it is nat forboden'; Lat. Et qui prohibet quibus prohibendum est et quibus non est prohibendum, avarus est.

[153] The English omits the rest of the link, excepting the speech of the last one of the several philosophers who engage in the discussion.

nature, it is not fitting that you acquire much; and if you wish to satisfy an avaricious mind, then, though you acquired everything on the face of the earth, the lust for gain will still burn within you." Another: "His wealth will last long who spends it sparingly." Another: "The source of peace is not to desire what belongs to another, and the fruit of it is to have rest." Another: "Whoever wishes to abandon life, let him see that he retain nothing that belongs to it, since only so much is worth while, unless he will extinguish the fire with dross." Another: "Whoever acquires wealth, works hard and languishes with watchfulness that he may not lose it; then he is wretched when he loses what he had acquired." The disciple to the master: "Do you praise the gaining of money?" The master: "Indeed! gain it; but spend it justly and for good purposes, and do not conceal it in your treasury."

And another philosopher saith: "Ne desire thow non other mans thyng and sorow thow nat of thynges lost, for of sorowe nothyng shalbe recoverable." Wherof he saith:

XVII[154]. THE CHURL AND THE BIRD

"Suche oon had a greene orchard or gardyn in whiche was moche and grete fuysoun of grene herbis. What shal I say ellis? Ther was a place also Right delectable in whiche ther gadred grete multitude of briddis with dyvers melodie of dyuers and many swete songes executyng.[155] Vpon a day while he for werynes Restid in his orchard suche a bridde (f. 130) sat vpon the tre, whiche that he sye and herd his voice and deceivaibely toke hym in a snare. To whom the brid: 'Why hastow laboured so moche to take me, or what profite hopistow to have in takyng of me?' [To this the man]: 'Only thi songes I desire to here.' To whom the brid: 'Triewly forwhi? for nothing price nor praier shal I syng.' Than he: 'But if thow syng I shal ete the.' And the brid: 'In what maner wilt[156] thow ete me? If thow ete me soden or bake what shal it availe of so litel a brid?'[157] And if I be Rosted moche lasse shal I be. But if thow wilt lete me go, grete profite therof wil folowe.' Quod he: 'What profite wil ther be therof?' The brid saide: 'I shal shewe the iii wisdam[158] that shuln availe the more than the flessh of iii calves.' And he folowyng the briddes promyse leete hym go. To whom the brid: 'Oon of the promises [is] that thow beleeve nor

---

[154] No. XXII in the original, I, 30, l. 26.
[155] This entire passage corresponds to the following sentence of the Latin (I, p. 30): Quidam habuit virgultum, in quo rivulis fluentibus herba viridis erat et pro habilitate loci conveniebant ibi volucres modulamine vocum cantus diversos exercentes.
[156] Ms. 'that' for 'wilt.'
[157] English omits Et etiam caro erit hispida.
[158] Lat. (I, 31, l. 8) sapientiae manerias.

trust nat to every man. The secunde is, that shalbe thyn alwey
thow shalt have. The thrid is, ne sorowe thow nat of thynges lost.'
This saide, the litel brid ascendid vpon the tree and with a sweete
voice bigan to synge: 'Blessid be god that hath shit and closed the
sight of thyn eyen and taken awey thi wisdam, forwhi if thow
haddest sought in the plites of myn entrailes thow shuldest have
founde a jacinct the weight of an vnce.' He heryng this bigan to
wepe and to sorowe and to smyte his brest with his fist for he yave
feith to the litel brid. And than the brid saide vnto hym: 'Thow art
soone foryetful of [the] wit of whiche I saide vnto the. Whether
I saide nat to the that thow shuldist nat beleeve everyman of that
he saith to the? And how belevistow that in me shuld be a jacynt
the weight of an vnce, whan I and al my body is nat of somoche
weight? And now I say to the that that thyn is alwey thow shalt have.
And how maistow have a stone in me a fleeyng foul? Now I saie
to the: ne sorowe thow never of thynges lost. And why sorowest
thow of the jacynct whiche in me is?' Suche thynges saide to grete
scorn to the Cherl the brid fligh awey to the woode."[159]

The philosopher chastised his son saying: "Read everything
that falls in your way but do not believe everything you read." To
this the disciple: "I believe this to be a fact: not everything that is
in books is true. For I have already read something like this in the
books and proverbs of philosophers: 'There are many trees but not
all of them bear fruit; there are many fruits but they are not all
edible'."

Arabs chasticed his sone saieng: "Sone ne leve thow nat thynges
present for thynges to come, forwhi haply thow shalt leese both as it
happened to the wolf of two promyses made to hym of the Cherl.

XVIII.[160] THE PLOWMAN WITH HIS OXEN AND THE WOLF AND THE FOX

"It is saide forwhi of a plowghman that for his oxen wold nat
drawe rightly, he saide the wolf shuld ete hem. The wulf heryng
that rested. Whan the day declyned to the nyght and the cherl
loosid his oxen out of the plowgh, the wulf cam vnto hym saieng:
'Yeve me thyn oxen whiche thow promisest (f. 130ᵇ). To this
the ploughman: 'If I saide so I affermed it nat with an oth.' And
the Wulf ageyn to hym: 'I ought to have that thow promysedest.'
Ther thei affermeden that it shuld come to iugement. That while
they maden thei metten with the Fox. To whom the wily fox saide

---

[159] The English omits the first paragraph of the connecting link as given in the
Latin version. See I, 31, l. 21.
[160] No. XXIII of the original, I, 32.

in their goyng: 'Whider tenden ye to go?' Thei than that was don told the fox. [To whom he] saide:[161] 'For nought ellis seeken yee a juge, forwhi therof I shal do rightwis iugement. But first suffre me to speke with oon of yow in counsail, and fro that with that other; and so I may make yow to accorde without a juge the sentence shalbe hid and clos. If forsoth otherwise incontynent be it saide.' And thei graunted; and the fox first abakk spak with the plowghman and saide: 'Gyve me an henne and another for my wif, and thow shalt have thyn oxen.' And the plowghman graunted; and this don the fox spake to the wulf saieng: 'Here thow, my friend, for thi merites and Rewardis bifore promysed as I ought if thei had bien myn owne, I have facundly somoche laboured and spoken with the Cherl that if thow wilt lete his oxen go quyte he shall yeve the a cheese to the gretnes of an helm made.' This don the wolf graunted. To whom the fox saide: 'Graunte thow the ploughman his oxen awey to leede, and I shal bryng the wher that his cheesis bien arraied and made, as that thow maist cheese of as many as thow wilt.' But the dul and foolissh wulf deceived bi the wordis of the fox, suffred the cherl to go. The fox forsoth wandryng hider and thider as moche as he myght, brought the wulf out of the ·wey. Whiche whan the derk nyght cam vpon, the fox brought the wulf to a diepe diche vpon whiche diche they stoode; the forme of, the half moone shewed and shyned in the bottom of the diche, and [he] saide: 'Here is the cheese which I promysed [the]. If it please the go doun and ete.' Quod the wolf: 'Go thow doun first and ete.' Than quod the fox:[162] 'Go thow doun first and if thow maist nat only bryng the cheese, I shal do as thow biddist'.[163] And this saide thei saw a corde hangyng in the diche in whos hede a litel possenet was bounde, and in that other hede of the corde another litel possenet. And thei hyng bi suche engyn and sleight that whan that oon aros that other went doun. That as the Fox sye, as to the praiers and besechynges of the wolf, entred in to the litel pot and cam to the bottum. The wolf therof was glad and saide: 'Whi bryngest me nat the cheese?' Quod the Fox: 'I may nat for the gretnes; but entre thow that other pot and come as thow saidest thow woldest.' The wolf entrying in to the pot with his gretnes anon asked and cam to the bottum, that (f. 131) other risyng with the fox whiche was glad. Whiche the litel fox whan he touched the mowth of the diche lept out and left the wolf in the diche. And

---

[161] Ms. 'What saide:' Lat. Quibus dixit.
[162] This sentence not in the Latin. See I, 32, 1. 21.
[163] Lat. Descende tu primitus, et si sola deferre non poteris, ut te iuvem faciam quae hortaris.

so for thyng to come [he] lost that was present: the wolf lost both oxen and cheese."

One sentence of the Latin connecting link is here[164] omitted the sense of which is: The Arab reproved his son saying: "Take counsel of that one who has experience in the thing thou askest about, for thou canst thus gain experience more easily than if thow makest the experiment thyself.

Svcheon chastised his sone [saying]: "Ne trust nat to the counsail that thow herist of al men lest it fal to the as it happened to the thief whiche trusted and trowed to the counsail of sucheon." To that the sone: "How cam it to hym, Fader?" Than the fader saide:

XIX.[165] THE THIEF AND THE MOONBEAM

"It is saide that suche a thief went to the house of suche a Richeman of entent to Robbe and stele; and ascended vp to the Roof and cam to the wyndowe or lover bi whiche the smoke went out and herkened if any withyn were awake. That whiche the lord of the house aperceived [and] saide softly vnto his wif: 'Aske and crie thow with an high voice whens it cam to me, the grete plente of money that I have. That as to cry and reherse laboure thow moche.' Than she with a grete voice saide: 'Sir, wherof hastow somoche money and thow wer never no Marchaunt?' [And he]: 'That god hath gyven kepe thow and do therof thi wil and aske nat wherof somoche money comyth.' And she, as she was enjoyned, more and more cried, reherced, and stired. Than he therof as coarted to the praiers of his wif saide: 'See that thow ne discovre oure counsail to any man; I was a thief.' Than saide she: 'It seemyth wonder to me how somoche money thow myghtest purchace and gete with theft and never I herd clayme ne chalange therof.'[166] Than saide he: 'Suche a Maister of myn taught me a charme that I shuld sey[167] whan I shuld ascende to the Roof of the house. And comyng to the wyndow I toke the beame of the Moone with myn hand and vii tymes saide my charme, that is to say, SAULE. And so I descendid and cam doun without perel, and what precious thyng I fond in the house I tooke it; and that don eftsones I cam to the beame of the Moone and the same charme vii tymes saide, with al that taken in the house I ascended and bare awey and brought to my howse. With suche engyne and wit I possede the money that I now have.' Than the wif saide: 'Thow

---

[164] I, 33, l. 3.
[165] No. XXIV in the original, I, 33, l. 8.
[166] Lat. Calumpniam inde.
[167] Ms. repeats 'whan that I shuld sey.'

didest weele of tho[168] thynges that thow hast saide and told to me; forwhi whan I have a sone I shal teche hym this charme that he shal nat neede to be poore.' And than the lord of the house saide: 'Suffre me now to sleepe for I am hevy of sleepe and wold rest.' And as somoche the more he mygt disceive the thief he snorted and Rented as he had bigonne to sleepe. And the thief[169] parceiving thoo wordis was glad and vii tymes saide the same charme and with his hand tooke the beame of the (f. 131b) Moone, straught out his handis and his feete from the wyndow, and fil in to the house, makyng a grete sowne and noise and with his bak and his arm broken lay wailyng. And the lord of the house as nat knowing [it] saide: 'Who art thow whiche fallist so?' To that the thief: 'I [am] an vnhappy[170] thief whiche trustid to thi fals and guylful wordis'."

To this the sone: "Fader, blissed be thow for thow hast taught me to beware of fals and gyleful counsail."[171]

(f. 135b) The philosopher: 'Biware the counsail of therf-brede til it be sowre dowgh.' Another: 'Ne bilieve the counsail that thow denyest of the moever of anothers goode dede, forwhi who that denyeth a goode deede bifore the eyen of hem all that hym biholdith hymsilf accusith.' Another: 'If thow be in any goodenes ne synne thow nat: kepe the,[172] for oftentyme the grettest goodenes is mynushid and made lasse or lost bi the lest'." The disciple asked his Maister: "Whether the philosopher forbedith a goode deede of his creator and maker or of his creature?"[173] To this the Maister: "I sey to the that he whiche denyeth a goode deede he denyeth god; and he whiche obeieth nat vnto his kyng and Ruler is disobedient vnto god." The disciple saide: "Shewe the reason how that may be." The Maister saide: "No goode deede procedit from creature to creature but it procede of god; and he the whiche denyeth a goode deede denyeth his benefactours and so he denyeth god, also the kyng whiche is Ruler and the veray trewe yerde of god is in erth."[174] Another philosopher saith: 'Kepe the from the kyng whiche is fiers

---

[168] Ms. 'that of tho.'

[169] Ms. 'thyng.'

[170] Ms. more like 'vphappy.'

[171] Part of the connecting link between this and the following exemplum, as the tales are arranged in the Latin (see I, 34), was taken out of its proper setting by the English translator, or by some copyist of the Middle English version, and shifted to the end of tale No. XXVII (No. XXXIV of the original and the real conclusion of the *Disciplina*), there serving as part of the connecting link between XXVII and XXVIII. In this reprint it is inserted where it naturally comes in the Latin.

[172] Lat. ne pecces serva.

[173] Lat. (I, 34, 1. 8) Prohibuit philosophus benefactum denegare; sed non divisit benefactum creatoris et creaturae?

[174] The Latin differs from the English in this sentence, Item: Rex qui rector verax est, virga Dei in terra est; et ille qui obedit virgae, obedit rectori; et ille qui non obedit virgae, non obedit Deo, I, 34, ll. 14-15.

as a lioun and light to wrath as a chield.' Another: (f. 136)
'Whiche saith evil of his king bifore the time of his deth'.* Another
saith: 'God suffrith lengger a synful kyng to Reigne in his persone
if he be goode and meke to his people than he doeth a iust kyng
in his persone if he be evil and cruel to his people.'[175]

Aristotil in his Epistel chasticed Alexander the kyng so saieng:
'Bettir it is with a fewe pesibly to Rule than to hold to grete
chivalry'.[176] Also: 'Hold Rightwise justice bitwene men and they
shuln love the; and array the nat[177] to yielde to any the borowed
chaunge of goode or evil, forwhi a friend shal abide the long'."[178]

XX.[179] CONCERNING MARIANUS

"Plato the philosopher rehersith[180] that suche anold kyng was
in Grece cruel to his peple. This grew and encreised in grete
werre of many of his elders.[181] Of whiche that he myght knowe the
comyng and hap therof he sent for al the philosophres of the
Regioun. Whiche whan thei wern gadred he saide: 'See yee a
how moche and how grete batail is to yow and to me, that for my
synne I trowe it is come to vs. But if any thyng is in me that is
reprehensible sey yee, and I shal hast me in yowre jugement to be
corrected.' Than the philosophers saiden: 'Of any crymes in yowr
body we knowe non, neither what to vs and to yow so comen we
wote nat. But here nygh vs[182] dwellith suche an old man whos name
is Maryne[183] whiche spekith with the holigost. To hym therfor send
yee sum men[184] by whom to vs what in al our lif is to come
he shal declare.' Thiese thynges don, he sent vnto hym vii
philosophres; whiche Citee in which he bifore dwelled thei entred.
of the whiche thei fond the most part desert. But they seekyng
his house, that is to say of Maryne, it was saide and told that he and
many of the Citezeins wern gon in to [the] wildernes. The philosophers heryng this went vnto hym; whiche and whom [when] the
wise man sawe he saide: 'Com yee, Com yee ambassatours and
legatis of the vnobedient kyng. Forsoth god hath yeven hym in to

---

*According to the Latin (I, 34, 1. 18) this is: 'Who speaks evil of the king shall die before his time.'

[175] Then we go back to f. 132b of the Worc. Ms., near the top of the page.

[176] Lat. (I, 34, 1. 22) magnam militiam tenere.

[177] Lat. nec properes.

[178] Lat. (I, 34, 11. 23-24) quia diutius expectabit te amicus et diutius timebit te inimicus.

[179] No. XXV of the original, I, 34, 1. 25.

[180] Lat. retulit in libro de prophetiis.

[181] Multis e partibus.

[182] Lat. Sed hic prope viam trium dierum.

[183] The four words beginning with 'whos' inserted on the margin of the Ms.

[184] Lat. de philosophis vestris aliquos.

the ward and kepyng of dyuers naciouns, forwhi he is no Right
Ruler nor gouernour but an enemy. God forsoth whiche hym and
his subiectis of the same and nat of dyvers matiers hath made and
formed, but his vnmoderate wikkidnes long while hath suffred and
with many correcciouns he hath monysshed and warned, as to be
torned and conuerted. But al vttirly only to the evil of his froward
soule of no noysaunce in to mercy of the barbaryus people and
nacioun hath areised.[185] And this saide the wiseman stilled. That
the philosophres heryng woundred and al tho that ther weren. The
iii day after the philosophers asked (f. 132) licence to go ageyn;
than that Reuerent with a spirite of prophecie saide vnto hem:
'Torne ye now ageyn forwhi yowre kyng is dede, and god now
ther hath set another kyng whiche shalbe a Rightful gouernour and
meke to al his people and subiectis.' Suche thynges herd of the vii
philosophers that com, iii of theym remayned and abode with this
wise man in [the] wildernes and iiii of theym went home ageyn in
to their cuntrey; whiche fonde al thynges as it was theym told and
saide."[186]

XXI.[187] ETIQUETTE IN THE KING'S SERVICE

[The fader] : "Who that wilbe seruaunt vnto a kyng ought to
see with al the sight of his mynde, than whan he comith to the kyng,
that he may long stonde ne never sitte til the kyng comaunde, nother
speke but whan it is neede; nother tary or abide but whan
the kyng comaundith hym to dwelle and abide, and his
counseil triewely kepe; and alwey be intentief to here what
the kyng saith, neither hym bihovith of this to aske the
kynges comaundement and whatsumever he comaundith do it;
but beware ne lie nat vnto thi kyng, and see that he love his kyng and
be to hym obedient; ne never associe ne felawship the nat with
noman that the kyng hatith or that he hatith the kyng.[188] And whan
he hath done al this and many another, haply [he] therby shal nat
have no grete profite of the kyng." Than the sone: "Nothyng worse

---

[185] This sentence is not at all clear in the translation because it is so inexact: Sed
tandem omnino ad malum eius pertinaci animo in illius necem immisericordes et barbaras
suscitavit gentes. See I, 35, 1. 13.

[186] Tale XXVI in the Latin is in reality about the wise merchant who refused to
settle in the country of a king whose expenses were as great as his income, which the
English translation reproduces as No. XXIV instead of XXI, as it would be in the
natural order of the dialogues. But No. XXI of the English version does reproduce a
part of the lengthy discussion between the Arab and his son concerning the proper
etiquette to be observed by any one in the service of a king, which follows No. XXVI
in the Latin (I, 36, 1. 26—p. 28, 1. 9.)

[187] No. XXVI, the concluding discussion of the original; the first part having been
shifted in the Middle English so as to form No. XXIV (which should, but does not,
correspond to No. XXIX of the original).

[188] Lat. has only quem rex odio habebit.

fallith or happenyth to a man than long to serve [the king] and no
goode to geete nor purchace." [The] Fader: "Many of thynges
now happenyth and cometh, and therfor the philosophre comaundith
that noman overmoche tary with his kyng nor in his seruice." And
another: "Who servith to the kyng without fortune so as I shal
sey he leesith this world?"[189] And the sone: "O fader, whi forye-
test thow to tel how a man ought to ete tofore a kyng?" [The
fader]: "I am nat foryetful to tel, forwhi no difference is to ete
before a kyng and elliswhere." The sone: "Say therfor how every-
wher a man ought to ete." [The fader]: "With vnwasshen handis
ne touche nor ete noon of thi lordis mete; ne ete thow no brede til
ther come another dissh vpon the table, ne speke thow nat vn-
paciently neither; only be ther noon grete embosyng[190] put in thi
Mowth, neither any crommes flowe or falle out;[191] and also behave
the that thow speke nat with swolowyng;[192] nother swolow thow no
morsel bifore that it be wele chewed in thi Mowth, lest thow be
strangled; ne take neither mete ne drynk[193] til thi Mowth be voide;
ne speke thow nat envi[n]ously;[194] ne speke thow nat while thow
holdist anythyng in thi mowth, neither any thyng entre in to the
throte in thyn inward arterie that myght be cause of thi deth; and if
thow see any thyng[195] in the dissh that pleasith the, ne take it nat
bifore thi felaw lest he say the to be shrewissh and cherolissh. After
mete wassh thyn handis, for it is phisik and curtesy; of this forsoth
(f. 132b) the eyen of many men bien empeired that after mete wipen
with vnwasshen handis." [The] Sone: "Whosoever biddith me to
mete, what shal I aunswer? Shal I graunt or nat?" The fader:
"Do thow as it is comaunded of the Jewis." He saith: "Forsoth who-
sumeuer biddith the, see thow the persone of the bidder. If he be
a worthy and a notable persone, anon graunt thow hym. Than if
he be nat after that it shalbe the thrid or the secunde tyme, and this[196]
is reherced of Habraham: Suche a day forsoth whan he stode
bifore his yaate [he] sawe goyng vnder mannes liknes iii Angels,
the whiche he praied to entre his house, their feete to wassh, re-
feccioun of mete to take, recreacioun and sport to make of their
werynes; and thus he praied theym with an honest chiere. Thei

---

[189] Lat. (I, 37, l. 3) hoc saeculum perdit et aliud.
[190] Lat. tantum bolum.
[191] Eng. omits ne dicaris gluto (I, 37, 10.)
[192] The Lat. (I, 37, l. 10) has nothing corresponding to this sentence.
[193] Lat. has simply nec pocula sumas donec, etc.
[194] Lat. ne discaris vinosus.
[195] Lat. bolum 'morsel.'
[196] Ms. 'this and'; Lat. (I, 37, l. 20) Hoc etiam.

forsoth as to a grete persone as he was, graunted anon to his peti-
cioun. Forsoth whan they comen to Loth, eftsones and eftsones
wern [thei] praied that thei shulden vndergo his Roof, for that he
was no grete persone; as coarted or driven of. soule thei wenten
away."[107] A yong [man] oones asked an old man: "Whan I am
boden to mete shal I ete moche?"[108] To whom thold man saide:
"Moche! forwhi if he be thi friend that bad the, he shal joye and
be glad of thi moche etyng; forsoth if he be an enemy he shal
sorow and be sorowful."[109] To whiche thold man saide: "What
and wherfor laughest thow, chield? For I am Remembred of the
wordis that I have herd of blac Maymund."

XXII.[200] THE LAZY SERVANT MAIMUND

"Suche an old man asked of hym hov moche he myght ete.
To whom he: 'Of whos mete? of myn mete or of another?' Quod
he: 'Of thyn.' Maymund: 'As litel as I may.' Quod he: 'What of
another?' [Maymund]: 'As moche as I may'." To whom thold
man: "Thow now remembrest of the wordis of sum gloton, slowth,
foole, jangler, or and a litel cat. And whatsumever of hym suche
be saide: this or that, more or lasse he fyndeth in hym."[201]
Tholdman: "His lord comaunded hym suche a nyght to shitte the
yaate; and he oppressed with slowth and vnlust myght nat arise and
therfor he saide the yaate was shit. Forsoth than in the Morow the
lord saide: 'Maymunde, open the yaate.' To whom the seruaunt
saide: '[Maister], I wist wel that thow woldest have it open this
day and therfor I shit it nat at eve.' Than the lord apperceived
that he left it vndon bicause of slewth and saide, 'Arise and do thi
werke for it is day and the Sonne is now high'. To whom the
seruaunt: 'If the sonne he at an height gyve me mete.' To whom
the lorde saide: 'Thow most worst seruaunt, wiltow ete the nyght?'
To whom the seruaunt: 'If it be nyght suffre me to sleepe.' Another
tyme the lord saide to his seruaunt in the nyght: 'Maymunde, arise
and see whether it Rayne or nat.' He forsoth cald the hounde
whiche lay without the gate and whan the dogge cam he felt his
feete that wern drye and saide to his lord that it Rayned nat.

---

[197] This is a very inexact translation; cf. I, 37, 25, quia autentica non erat
persona, velut coacti annuerunt.

[108] Lat. quid faciam: parum vel nimis comedam?

[199] The English omits Hoc audito risit puer 'When the boy heard this he laughed.'

[200] No. XXVII in the Latin, I, 38, l. 3.

[201] The English omits the following sentence of the Latin (I, 38, l. 7): Iuvenis:
Multum placet mihi de eo audire, quia quicquid de eo est, derisorium est; et si quid
de eius dictis vel factis mente retines, eloquere, et habeo pro munere. The young man:
"I am greatly pleased to hear about him, for everything about him is ridiculous; and
if you remember any of his sayings and actions, tell me and I shall have my reward."

Another tyme the lord asked his seruaunt in the nyght (f. 133) if
any fuyre were in the house. He forsoth cald the cat and tempted
hir whether she were hote or nat, whiche whan[202] he fond cold saide
to his lord ther was noon."

[The Yongman] : "Of the yongman his slowth now have I herd
and the jangler I coveite to here." Than thold man: "It is saide
that his lord cam glad from the market for the moche wynnyng
that he had there. And Maymund the seruaunt went out agenst his
lord; whom whan his lord saw, [he was] crymynous lest any shrewd
tidynges [he would tell], as he was wont to tell, [and] saide vnto
hym: 'Beware thow tel me no shrewd tidynges.' The seruaunt
saide: 'I shal tel the no shrewde tidynges; but, sir, Bispel our litel
dog is dede.' To whom the lord: 'How is he dede?' The seruaunt:
'Our Mule was agast and brake his halter[203] and trade the hounde
vndir his feete and so hath slayn hym.' The lord: 'And what is don
of the Mule?' The seruaunt saide: 'He fil in the diche and is
dede.' The lord than: 'How was the Mule gasted?' Than the
seruaunt: 'Yowre sone fil from the solier above so that he is dede,
and so was the Mule gasted.' Than the lord: 'What dide his Moder?'
The seruaunt: 'For the grete sorowe of hir sone she is dede.' The
lord: 'Who kepith the house?' The seruaunt: 'Noon, forwhy it is
torned into asshen and what ellis that was therin.' The lord: 'How
was it brent?' The seruaunt: 'The same nyght that my lady deide,
the foote Maiden whiche wacchid for my lady was foryeteful and
left the candel in the Chamber and so thyn house is brent.' The
lord: 'Wher is the footemayde?' The seruaunt: 'She wold have
qwenched the fuyre and[204] fil vpon hir hede and is dede.' The
lord: 'How escapest thow whiche art so slow?' The seruaunt:
'Whan I saw the foote maide dede I fled.'

Than the lord wounder sorowful cam to his neighburghs
praieng hem to host and herburgh hym in sum howse. In the meane
while he mette oon of his friendis, whiche whan he saw hym sorowful asked hym why he sorowed. He to hym reherced that his seruaunt had saide. The friende forsoth to the desolate friende reherced ageyne, sayeng as to make hym myrry: 'Friende, nyl thow
be nat desolate ne sory, forwhi often tymes fallen to a man many
worldly aduersitees that thoo thynges desirith and with honest deth
to fynissh; and anoon suche comodites comen vnto hem that the
more redier swetnes be to hym to Remembre of the aduersitees

---

[202] Ms. 'whom.'
[203] The English omits the following clause, dum fugeret.
[204] Lat. (I, 39, l. 6) et cecidit trabs super caput eius, and a beam fell on her head.

past.'²⁰⁵ But thiese kyndly thynges as wel in vnmesurable floteryng
variaunce of merites with ordynaunce of the high Ruler distinctith
to arbitrement.²⁰⁶ This and the prophete Job strenghed to en-
sample of whos soule was nat devoured with losse of thynges.²⁰⁷
Whether hastow nat herd what the philosopher saith: 'Who may in
this chaungeable world be any thyng stable, or who may in this
lif any thyng to have enduryng while and whan thei bien so transitory'?"

The Arabik to (f. 133ʰ) his sone: "Sone, whan any aduersite
fallith to the, nyl thow be to sorowful neither therof be in to moche
desolacioun, for this is nat the kynde nor the maner to denye god.
But thow oughtest to praise god, as wele of adverse as of pros-
perite. Forsoth many evils fallen to men whiche that comen as to
eschewe and flee the more and the gretter evils; and many [evil]
thynges fallen whiche enden in goode. And therfor thow ougtest to
praise [god] in al thynges and, in hym to trust, as the versifiour
saith: 'Whan thow art in sorow nyl thow be busy therof, but per-
mytte and suffre the tyme in goddis disposicioun and tel ageyn alwey
the goodenes to com; and so shaltow be foryeteful of evils, forwhi
many evils comen whiche han a goode end.' The philosopher saith:
'The goodis of this world bien eveene myxt and medled. Forsoth
thow etest no hony without venym.' Another 'Whatsumever bien
in the world bien chaungeable; and what goodis thow hast of hem
thei bien to come to the though it be or thow feeble be and of evil
streng this thow mayst nat withstande.'²⁰⁸

Another: 'Because they allow a slow person to obtain what he
desires, they also refuse a swift person the obtaining of his.'

Another: 'He hymself beawtith the world with fairness and bi
that he hath wonne that he wold the erth hym swolowith and de-
vourith.' Another: 'As in a twynklyng of an eye endith the glorie
and joies of the world; and as so free al abidith now, he seeth
nat of thynges obteyned'."

²⁰⁵ This sentence is a good example of the translator's crude, inartistic work and his insufficient knowledge of the Latin (I, 39, l. 11): Amice, noli desolari, quia multo-tiens contingit homini tam graves adversitatum inundationes sustinere quod desideret eas etiam inhonesta morte finire; et statim eveniunt ei tanta commoda quod prorsus dulce sit ei praeteritarum reminisci adversitatum.

²⁰⁶ Lat. (I, 39, l. 14) Sed humanarum rerum tam immensa fluctuatio variante meri-torum ordine summi rectoris distinguitur arbitrio.

²⁰⁷ Lat. prophetiae Iob corroborantur exemplo: cuius animum non pessumdedit amis-sio rerum.

²⁰⁸ Lat. (I, 40, ll. 1-2) et quae ex eis tibi bona sunt ventura, licet sis debilis, et malum viribus devitare non poteris. In the English version the speech of the next philosopher is omitted (Lat. 40, l. 3.):

XXIII.[209]   SOCRATES (DIOGENES) AND THE KING.

Forsoth proverbialy thei seyn that Socrates eschewid the tumult
and the multitude of worldly people and a fieldly lif coveited, chase
hym to the woode and to a place of sikernes to dwelle in half a
Tonne; of whiche the bottum he sette agenst the wynde and the
shadewe, and that was open gladly agenst the Sonne. Whom the
kynges hunters, whan they had founden scornede hym sleyng his
life, bigan to turne awey the myrry beames of the sonne. To whom
he with a glad chiere [saide] : 'That ye may nat yeve me presume
nat to take awey.' To that thei wrathed and hym to delaie that hym
nedid wolden have compelled and out of the wey han led, lest that
the eyen of men passyng by and of their lord so vile a persone
shuld have offended. That nat the threatis or manaces of worthy
men [saide] : 'Avoide and go, lest of thy long studie and busynes any
evil vnto the happene, forwhi our kyng with his seruaunt and
meyne is to passe this wey.'[210]   Thei forsoth in hym berkyng and
threateyng the philosopher biholdyng saide :[211] 'Yowre lord is nat
my lord but my seruaunt.' That heryng and with a newly chiere
hym biholdyng, sum decre thei purposiden of lasse Reproef and
threate til thei herden the sentence of the kyng thei decreeden.[212]
Forsoth while thei thus decreeden the kyng cam with his meyne,
and what was the cause of (f. 134) the strif askyng, what deedis
wern don or saide, the kynges seruauntis rehercyng he knewe it.[213]
The kyng therfor willyng to knowe what of tho foule thynges to
hym reherced wern aught feyned, to the philosopher than he went
and inquiryng what the philosopher saide of hym. So as bifore
vnto his meyne, so hym assured to be seruaunt of his seruauntis.
The sentence of whiche wordis the kyng benyngly and with a dili-
gent trust asked hym to tel and shewe. To whom the philosopher
bihielde the face and chiere of his dignite lightly saide : 'Suche wil is
seruaunt vnto me and to me servith and I nat to hym. And thow
in the contrarie art subiect vnto wil and to hym thow servist, and

---

[209] No. XXVIII in the original, I, 40, l. 8.

[210] The corresponding Latin for this sentence is (I, 40, l. 14) Quod non valentes
minati sunt ei dicentes: Vade ne quid mali ex protervitatis studio tibi contingat, quia
rex noster et dominus cum familiaribus suis et primitibus est hac parte transiturus.

[211] Lat. Illos autem in se latrantes philosophus intuens.

[212] The words of this sentence are quite distinct in the Ms., but the meaning is
obscure. The Latin (I, 40, l. 18) runs, Quod audientes et novercali vultu eum respicientes
quidam eum detruncare proposuerunt, minus vero improbi donec sententiam regis
audirent, parcere ei decreverunt.

[213] In this sentence again we have a specimen of the crudest translation of the
Latin, in which the literal meanings of the words are occasionally set down without
any apparent connection with what precedes or follows, Dum vero in hunc modum decer-
tarent, rex adveniens et quae causa litigii foret perquirens, quae gesta fuerant vel
dicta famulis referentibus cognovit.

nat he to the. Therfore thow art seruaunt of hym whiche servith me.' Than the kynge fixed a litel his sight in to the erth and saide: 'Fader, ne shamest thow nat nor gastest of my power?'[214] To whom the philosopher in the straytnes tooke his seete[215] and saide: 'Knowe thow hym to the to grete abusioun to have lordship of mortal thynges and the matier of thynges bryngyng the to opteyne whiche nat with thi vertu or strength, nor stilliche thow doest it of eveene consent, but of glorious covetise as the chiernes of the thyng is thow hast don to be lawded and praised whiche that is exiled and voide of al the weight.[216] So considre thow thi glorie that is past and thi power as may be now as nought nor to be drad; but neither of thynges to come, of whos hap or comyng is doutable and vncerteyn. Thus it owith of this present lif forwhi it is but litil and momentaneous and whiche in the twynklyng of an eye is brought to nought.'[217] He perceivyng the wordis of the philosopher, the kyng saide to his meyne: 'Forsoth he is the seruaunt of god! See yee that yee do hym noon hurt nor non vnhonest thing.'"[218]

XXIV.[219] THE WISE MERCHANT AND THE IMPROVIDENT KING

"Forsoth it is saide that suche a kyng of the Scites[220] bi the comune assent of his nobles to suche on of his seruauntis whom thei cald Anne[221] to be prudent and wise in seculier and worldly thynges; al the bridels and Rulis of his Realme to hym he commytted, whiche al the Revenues and Rentis of the Realme he Received and plesauntly and pesibly entreatid, the house and the household meyne and Ministres seruauntis and their dispenses ordeyned. A Riche Marchaunt his brother in a Citee fer of indwellid. The which perceived bi Rumour and tidynges of his brother enhauncyng and pro-

---

[214] Lat. (I, 41, l. 2) Ut patet in verbis tuis, nihil meae potentiam gloriae vereris.

[215] Lat. in angustam suae mentis sedem receptus.

[216] Lat. (I, 41, l. 3) Scis ipse nimium tibi ambitionem rerum mortalium dominatam fuisse et materiam gerendis rebus te optavisse, quo ne virtus tua ut ipse fateris consenesceret tacita; sed ob cupidinem gloriae sicut rei sinceritas est fecisti adipiscendae. quae gloria quam sit exilis et totus vacua ponderis, sic considera. Tuae praeteritae gloriae potentia utpote, et cet.

[217] The English omits the final clause of the rather long sentence of the original, ob hoc ergo in nulla parte sui est formidanda, 'for this reason therefore it is in no respect to be dreaded for its own sake.'

[218] In the Latin version this tale is followed by a discussion of the end of life (De vitae termino) between the master and his disciple. And a small part of the connecting dialogue is not given in the English translation; but in the English version what is reproduced has been transferred from its original place (between XXVIII and XXIX) and inserted after No. XXIV corresponding, not to XXIX of the Latin, which would be the natural order, but to No. XXVI.

[219] No. XXVI of the original, I, 35, l. 23.

[220] This word is not in the Latin, which runs: Dictum namque fuit quod quidam rex suorum, et cet. See I, 35.

[221] This word might be 'Aime' or 'Amie' in the Ms.; but even so there is nothing corresponding to it in the Latin, either in meaning or in form, but 'antea,' the sentence being cuidam suo familiari, quam antea cognoverat in saecularibus esse prudentem.

motyng, arraied a felawship as it bihoved as to visite his
brother [and] bigan his jorney.   Only bifore [he] sent a messenger lest that sodainly or vnprovided [he] shuld come; whiche told
of his brothers comyng to a Citee that was ther nygh.[222]   He heryng
of his brother, the brother mette hym and with a glad chiere hym
tooke and (f. 134b) resceived.   Than after past a fewe daies, place
and tyme purveied whiche he knewe pleasaunt vnto hym, among
other thynges rehersed vnto the kyng his brothers comyng.   To
whom the kyng: 'If thi brother wil dwel and Rest with the in my
Realme, al my thynges to the with hym I shal betake to kepe.   And
though that he denye it, yet I shall yeve and graunt hym large possessiouns in this Citee; and al the customs that he ought to do vnto
me I shal pardon hym.   If forsoth from that only bi touche or
feelyng of love natural [he] wil go ageyn in to his cuntrey, with
many chaunge of vestymentis and whatsumever ellis to hym
necessarie with habundance I shal enlarge.'   The wordis of the
kyng herd, the brother cam to the brother and as moche as his lord
had hym promysed to hym he told and reherced.   To whom the
brother: 'If thow wilt that I dwel with the, shewe me how moche
bien the Rentis of the kyng and his Revenues.'   He forsoth shewid
hym al.   Of that he askid hym what was the kynges expenses; and
he told hym of that he made.   Than he accompted that the kynges
expenses was as moche as the Rentis and Revenus amounted; and
[he] saide vnto his brother: 'Friend and brother, I see that the
kynges dispenses bien as moche as his Rentis.   And if yowre kyng
areised any bataile or any other suche thyng like, wherof shalbe
procured for his knyghtis or wherof shal their wagis bien founde?'
[The] Brother: 'Therof we shuln seeke other counsail.'   To whom
the brother: 'I dreede me if I shuld be partyner[223] of this maner
counsaile, and therfor farwele, for here I wil no more ne lenger
dwell'."[224]

"Svche a philosopher saith: 'To werke for the world to come as
thow now shuldest die, and so as for this present world thow were
alwey to lyve.   Forsoth it is bettir that after thi deth thyn enemyes
have thi purchace than that thow live needily in this lif.'   Another

---

[222] Lat. (I, 36, l. 1) Praemisso tandem nuntio, ne subitus aut improvisus veniret,
qui de avdentu suo fratri referret, civitati in qua frater aderat appropinquavit.

[223] Lat. (I, 36, l. 16) Timeo ne census meus sit pars huius consilii.

[224] Now, the English translator inserts a portion of the dialogue which connects
tales XXVIII and XXIX in the Latin after No. XXIV; but he omits the beginning of
the discussion about the end of life (see 1, 41, l. 12): Again the disciple said to his
master: "Since worldly things are so transitory, why should we make just as great
preparations as if they were lasting?"   The master: "Because the end of life is uncer-
tain."   At this point the English version takes up the argument again.

saith: 'The world is transitorie; of that therfor with honeste provide to the althynges necessary, forwhi the cours of lif is but short.' Another saith: 'The world is as a transitorye brigge, therfor bihold it nat. The world is a stable brigge whos entre is the wombe of the Moder and deth shalbe thissue of the same'."[225]

A versifiour saith: 'Deth is a yaate openyng and shewyng al erthely thynges bi the wey; but I seeke after this whiche is the house of habundaunce.' Ther is an house of delices to goddis seruauntis and ther is an house of derknes to theym that deserven peynes.'[226]

The Arab asked his father: "How can I acquire the home of delights and the fame of that one?" The father: "Whatever dear and precious things you possess, deposit them for safe-keeping there and when you come thither, they will be ready for you." The son: "How can I entrust money to a house, the door of which I can not yet find?" The father: "Hear what the son of the king's counsellor did after his father's death." The son: "Father, tell me and I will not refuse to follow your counsel." The father: "A certain king had a wise counsellor and servant, who at his death left a young heir well instructed in the ways of court life. To him he left his entire estate which was large, and an abundance of riches and then died. After this the king summoned the boy to him and informed him of the death of his father, that he might not grieve more sorely, and whatever the father by his testament left under his control for the son he assured him of, and in addition he promised that he would take him into his father's place when he became of age. Thereupon the youth bade the king farewell and joyously went to his own home. The king then forgot about him, and he was in no haste to return to the king. After a long time, the people in the district in which the boy lived began to be in such great want that they were in danger of death by famine. The youth saw this and he was much grieved in spirit, because he was of a generous nature, and so he emptied his granaries and distributed the contents among the poverty-stricken people; he also gave bountifully of his stock of wine and meat to those in distress. And as the suffering increased his decreasing resources were not sufficient to supply the wants of the needy. And afterwards, though he did not hesitate to give his fortune for grain. so as to save the lives of the laboring people from hunger and thirst as much as he could, that was still not sufficient. He did the same thing with his clothes and jewelry. And thus the period of a year passed in which he rescued many people from the very jaws of death. There was also in the same locality a certain amanuensis of the king, who filled with envy towards the youth, was secretly stirring

---

[225] The translator has omitted a few important words in the original and thus made the meaning somewhat confusing (see I, 41, l. 19), Alius: Saeculum et quasi pons: transi ergo, ne hospiteris. Et alius: Saeculum est quasi pons instabilis: cuius introitus est matris uterus, et eiusdem mors erit exitus.

[226] The rest of the connecting dialogue in the Latin (see I. 41, l. 25 and 42) and the immediately following tale (No. XXIX, *The Wise Son of the King's Counsellor*) are omitted from the English.

up bitter hostility against him. This fellow tried to exasperate the
king against the boy by some such words as these: 'Master, your
majesty's moderation towards the son of your former counsellor,
whose father left him an inexhaustible supply of money was very
weak, not to say foolish; for now neither you nor he have the
money, because he, silly youth, has squandered it.' The king, moved
to anger by such words, sent a messenger for the young man, to
whom he spoke as follows: "Foolish son of a wise man, idle and
lavishly extravagant, why hast thou wasted the wealth acquired by
wisdom which was entrusted to thy keeping?" To this the youth
replied with dejected countenance—for he feared the face of his
chief, inflamed as it was, with eyes flashing furiously: "Master, if I
may speak with your favor, I am not, as it seems to certain people,
a foolish son entrusted to you by a wise father. My father did
indeed gain wealth, and he placed it where thieves might steal it,
in that he left it to me from whom you could take it, or fire could
burn it or any accident destroy it. But I have bestowed it where it
will be faithfully kept for him and for me." And the king asked
what he had done with it. The youth related to him all his care in
disposing of his wealth, and when the king heard his story he praised
his actions highly in the presence of his attendants, and then received him into the service formerly done by his father as recompense. He afterwards gained new wealth and acquired greater
riches than he formerly possessed. It was in this way that the noble
son of the king's counsellor stored away treasure in his home of
delights."

After the son heard these words of his father he said: "That
youth acted wisely and gave evidence that great nobility was to be
manifested in him. He did as the philosopher who advised his son,
saying: 'Son, sell this world for the future, and you will gain both.'
And so it happened."[227]

Another saith: "See yee lest yee bien disceived for worldly
delites and broken with worldly fallaces and guyles and bien foryeteful of deth to come, lest it fal to the as it fil to the thief entryng
(f. 135) the house of the Richeman." To whom the sone and of the
fader:[228] "What fil therof, fader?" [The fader]:

XXV.[229] THE THIEF CAUGHT WHILE HESITATING ABOUT WHAT TO TAKE

"The thief entrid the house of the Richeman and fond it ful of
dyvers juels and precious thynges. Of this astonyed of the many
dyvers diversitees and so precious Riches charged hymsilf for to

---

[227] After this the English version returns to the dialogue which connects No.
XXVIII (of the Latin) with No. XXIX, but it omits the first speech of the dialogue,
Another correcting his son said: "Son work for the future life before death removes
thee from work."
[228] Lat. Ede, pater.
[229] No. XXX of the original, I, 43, l. 9.

chese of the most Richest; and tho that wern most vile levyng and forsakyng, and in his choise wasted tyme til the day cam, what that he wol do he hid. And vnavised the wacche cam vpon and bihield the thief in the house in cheesyng of the juels and hym with battis, habergeouns, and staves toke²³⁰ and cast hym in diepe prisoun. At the last date as now of his confessioun he herd the bittir stories and sentence of his hede; whiche if he had bifore thought of his day so nygh to come, or that shuld have befalle, he wold han beware that he wold nat have be taken nor have lost his hede."²³¹

Another [philosopher] saide: "The Richessis of this world bien transitorie as the dreames of a slepyng man, the whiche wakyng in openyng of his eyen vnrecoverably he hath lost."²³²

"A certain shepherd dreamed he had a thousand sheep. These a certain dealer wishing to buy so that he could sell them at a profit, offered to pay a dollar for each sheep. But the seller demanded a dollar and a quarter. While they were disputing about the price the dream vanished. But when the vender discovered that it was a dream he began to shout, with eyes not yet open: 'Give me a dollar for each and you may take them all with you!'

But while they pursue in this manner the transitory joys of the world and are with gaping mouths trying to secure them, suddenly the approaching day, the final one of life, overtakes them and deprives them willy-nilly of all desired pleasures."

Then the son: "Can we then escape, in any way, our obligations to death?" The father: "Not at all; because its grasp is unavoidable, and we can not even with the skill of the physician escape from its greedy clutches." The son: "How shall we then bear up under this too great suffering?" The father: "Do as a certain poet says: "Endure with strong heart what you can not shun, so shall what was harsh death be peaceful to you'."²³³

"It is told of a certain philosopher that he saw, as he was passing through an old graveyard, a marble slab placed over the ashes of a certain dead man; but on it were inscribed verses which expressed in the following manner the words of the dead man to passersby: 'Thou who passest by and dost not say, 'Blessed,' pause; keep these words of mine in thy ears and heart: I am what thou wilt be, and what thou now art I was once myself,—a scorner of bitter death who enjoyed happiness while I could. But death coming later I was snatched away from my friends and household, which is now grievously deprived of its father, whom they covered

---

²³⁰ Ms. 'hym toke.'
²³¹ English omits vel quod gravius extitit.
²³² There is nothing in the English version corresponding to the two immediately following short exampla of the original. The first of these (see I, 43) is entitled *About the Shepherd and the Dealer* (XXXI,, *Exemplum de opilione, et mangone*); it embraces only a few lines.
²³³ The second of the tales missing from the English version at this point, No.-XXXII, is entitled *Concerning the Philosopher Crossing the Cemetery* (*Exemplum de philosopho per cimiterium transeunte.* Cf. I, 44.)

in the ground, and they paid the last rites to my ashes. But then the earth spoiled the brightness of my face, and all the mortal beauty of my form now lies here. Thou canst not even see that I was a man, if I perchance be exposed to view by the removal of the earth. Therefore pray to God for me with a pure heart, that he will permit me to enjoy eternal peace. And whoever prays for me let him request that he also be allowed to abide with me in paradise.' When he had repeated those verses again and again and had laid all worldly things aside, the philosopher was made a hermit."

XXVI.[234] THE SAYINGS OF THE PHILOSOPHERS AT THE TOMB OF ALEXANDER THE GREAT

"It is saide of Alisaunder that his sepulture was al of gold and[235] in a litel porche sette. To whiche cam many philosophers, of the whiche oon saide: 'Alisaunder made his tresour of gold; and now the contrarie, gold makith tresour of hym.' Another saide: 'Yisterday al the world sufficied hym nat; and this day only iiii cubites sufficen hym.' Another saide: 'Yisterday he empired and lordshipped the people; and this day the people lordshippith hym?' Another saide:[236] 'Yesterday he pressid therth; and this day the erth pressith hym.' Another saide: 'Yisterday the people dred hym; this day thei deputen hym vile.' Another saide: 'Yisterday he had friendis and enemyes; this day he hath equal and evene.' But of xxxii philosophers standyng aboute hym, that eueriche of the myghti kyng saide is to be brought in long memory."

XXVII.[237] THE HERMIT CHASTENING HIS SOUL

"Also an heremyte and philosopher in this maner correctid his soule and saide: 'Soule, wite thow and knowe thow while power is in the and in thyn hand, that thow werke and do bifore that thow moevist from thi place to the house in whiche right and justice dwellith and abidith, and to the yaate of the place wher thow shalt trede in a Rolle whatsumeuer thyn hand hath don and wrought in this world.[238] And angels of hevene on thi Right and lift side shuln discovere, open, shewe, and tel thi counsail; and what goode

---

[234] No. XXIII of the original, see I, 44-45.

[235] Ms. 'and and.'

[236] Between this speech and that of the preceding philosopher the English version omits the sayings of two philosophers, Alius: Heri multos potuit a morte liberare: hodie nec eius iacula valuit devitare. Alius: Heri ducebat exercitus: hodie ab illis ducitur sepulturae.

[237] No. XXIV of the original, I, 45, l. 9.

[238] For latter half of this sentence the Latin is, et ad portam loci iudicii, ubi leges in rotulo quicquid tua manus egerit in hoc saeculo.

or evil thow hast don[239] in any of the same shalbe clierly ex-
amyned,[240] and al thi brethren and friendis shuln nat fynde no
redempcioun nor maynprice, and of this and from the vttirly de-
parten and forsaken. Therfor this day take thow redempcioun;
oo goode deede do thow bifore that the day of somounce come. Be
thow turned vnto god and say nat (f. 135ᵇ), "I shalbe torned to-
morow."[241] forwhi so morowly[242] and daily[242] concupiscence shal lette
the and haply withold the in to the last day. Therfor remembre and
have mynde of the daies of the world and of the yeeris of old gene-
raciouns whiche now bien past, and therof take thow wit and feele.
Wherbe now princis, wherbe now kynges, wherbe now Riche men
that gadreden tresours and therof wern thei prowde? Now bien
they as whiche ne weren; now bien thei as a flour or a blossum
whiche that is fallen from the tree whiche no more cometh ageyne.[243]
Ne dreede thow nat, my soule, ne drede thow nat to moche the
aduersites of the worlde. Dreede the day of thi jugement. Be agast
and abasshed of the grete multitude of thi synnes. Have mynde of
thi creator and maker whiche shalbe thi juge and thi witnes.'

Suche an heremyte asked of his master: 'What shal I do in
this that may go bifore me in another world?' Than the Maister:
'Do the goode that is to be don in thi degre and kynde.' Another
Heremyte cried bi the strete:[244] 'Ne trowe ne trust nor bilieve to
thynges foryeteful for to have durabilite of thynges in thend.'
Another sowned and saide: 'Love and profite asmoche to yowr
soulis as to yowre bodies.' Another: 'Foryete yee nat that
that foryetith nat yow and kepe yee to governaunce.' Another:
'Dreede yee god, forwhi the dreede of god is the key to al goode-
nesse and to take the glorious conduct. Of the whiche Salamon
puttith and settith in thend of his speche:[245] "Al thynges redily and
toguydre here we: 'Dreede thow god and kepe his comaundementis.'
to this is everyman. And al thynges that thei don shalbe brought to
goddis iugement for every synne, be it goode or evil'."[246]

---

[239] The English omits the last clause of the sentence preceding this and the first of
the present sentence itself as compared with the Latin: et quicquid a te fuerit excogi-
tatum. Et ante Deum veniet tuum iudicium, and whatever shall have been thonght by
thee. And thy judgment shall come before God.

[240] Lat. et una lance quicquid boni et alia quicquid mali egeris, sed uno et eodem
declarabitur examine. Cf. I, 45.

[241] The sentence structure in this passage is quite different from that of the Latin,
Hodie itaque redemptionem accipe, id est: bonum fac assidue. Et antequam veniat dies
summonitionis, ad Deum revertere et non dicas: cras revertar et non morabor, quia sic
crastinantem, et cet. See I, 45, l. 16.

[242] Both these words are given as interpretation of crastinantem.

[243] Eng. omits clause of Latin immediately preceding this: mode sunt finiti sicut
qui non vixerunt, now they have ceased to exist as those who never lived.

[244] Lat. per vicos.

[245] Lat. in Ecclesiaste ait.

[246] After this sentence which concludes the story in the Latin, there are four or
five lines of Epilogue.

Let us therefore as suppliants pray constantly for the great mercy of the omnipotent God, in order that we may by means of our good works deserve to be placed after the day of final judgment on the right hand of his Son, to enjoy eternal rest in the heavenly home together with the faithful in the presence of our Lord Jesus Christ, to whom are honor and glory with the Father and the Holy Spirit throughout the infinite ages. Amen.[247]

XXVIII.[248] THE KNIGHT IN EXILE AND HIS FRIEND WHOSE WIFE PLAYED HIM FALSE

Svche a knyght of his cuntrey of many hasty enemyes convict of his prevy synnes iuged to the deth, but withe kynges saieng and of the people knowen soone from the people was he exiled. And forwhi he left to hym no friend owther in the cuntrey or in thendis of the cuntrey, fled fer of wher nat only the act of his wikkednes but moche wors it was to hem purposed an vnknowen name with a laudable novelte thold cruelte and mansuete and the vndouted intemperat strength to converte and turne. Applied hymsilf to suche a myghti man, to whom so prudently is infelawshipped, and as of the Subiectis of that lord he myght be leest anoied and to hymsilf most profite, while and whan thei promytted plentevously as moche feith and lasse noied than dide vnkynde cruelte, and while tho open signes bitokened moche more power than he myght do. Forsoth he had in the same felawship a felawe of high vertu, a man the whiche with symilitude and liknes of vertu chosen, asked hym as in friendship thei myghten come. He nat denyed, an oth[249] halwed and rightfully to swere friendship and covenaunt affermed and stidefastly to be comuned[250] and commune to wynnyng and losse. [And he] bitooke and lad that exul his felaw in to his Citee. Forsoth willyng with hym to comune, his wif separat brought he[251] to

---

[247] Cf. I, 46. The English version has nothing correpsonding to this epilogue and does not end here, but continues the discussion of the philosophers for several paragraphs more, cf. above p. 65, footnote 246. Then the three additional tales mentioned above (*Introd.* p. 11, footnote 9) are given without the usual philosophic discussions which link together the preceding exampla.

[248] (The following three tales were printed by Hilka and Söderhjelm (*op. cit. I.* Anhang ii, pp. 68-73) with the corresponding Latin from Cambr. Univ. Libr. Ms. li. 6. 11 in parallel columns. The second one of the three (No. XXIX) was also printed by the present writer in vol. XXIV (Nov. 1909, pp. 218-22) of *Mod. Lang Notes* (*A Middle English Addition to the Wager Cycle*). The present text has been carefully. collated with the rotograph of the original Ms. The Hilka-Söderhjelm text is on the whole reliable, though it contains a considerable number of mistakes of minor importance. Each case in which my own transcript differs from their reprint I have settled by reference to the original.

[249] H. & S. read 'quoth'; but the Ms. has 'an oth', which suits the context, and the Latin agrees: Non abnegavit ille: sanctita est inreiurando amiscicia et. cet. I, 69, ll. 4-5.

[250] H. & S. incorrectly 'stedfast....communed.'

[251] Ms. 'hym.'

host, nor [252] shewed hym his house.[253] Forsoth the same Citee hasted from thendis, but the vertu and strength of theym was but a fewe daies. That exul or exiled man shewid to his felaw triewly[254] of the eveen partis of al the lucre and wynnynges. Whan also that pees was made and don in the Citee, sumtyme he allone walkyng bi the stretis[255] biholdyng gold and silver made and hostriches and hors of bataile from anhigh, of the wif of his felaw was seen and most brennyngly of hir loved, and is required as that same nyght he come to hir bi the message of hir footemaide. He cam and went ageyn with grete weight of gold and many precious stones awey bare. Whan that this lucre he departed to his felawe, whor[256] that he had it shewed and told, advertisyng he and his wif to be corrupt and his money to be mynnised.[257]

To that he the lord of the house symuled and feyned hymsilf to go fer of, vnavisede to be. Vnder the barel in whiche the habergeoun[258] was wont to be torned happened thadvoutrer ther was hidde and (f. 136b) busily sought and nat founde. Whan the lord was wery, he and the wif laughed that he hield so long and knocked on the barel next whom he stoode; neither it perced[259] nor opened and the felaw a litel felt. After that the grutche ended and he gon, with more charge left the knyght the secunde tyme than at the first. The lucre eveene patid, [thei] arraied theym eftsones with sawtis and watches to go ageyn and hid was bihynde the chambre dore and nat founde. And so parted the lucre. The thridde tyme watches and sawtis arraied, he was cast in an huche ful of clothis chaungeable.[260] Whan that he wolde seeke with a constant chiere and a stidefast face to his entent, she consented. Saide only hymsilf that he wolde entre as to knowe to drawe, wrappe, and folde the clothis and also to shape and olde clothis and fumous[261] to breke and so by space of tyme covered, protect and defended the advoutrier. The whiche nat[262] founde sorowyng he departed. The knyght [is sent

---

[252] Ms. 'nat.'

[253] Lat. I, 69, ll. 7-8. Nolens ei communicare uxorem suam in separatum duxit hospicium, domo sua nequaquam ei ostensa.

[254] H. & S. 'traewly.'

[255] H. & S. 'strietis.'

[256] H. & S. 'whar,' Ms. clearly 'whor.' Lat. (I, 69, 1. 21) unde haberet indicavit.

[257] Ms. might be 'mynused' or 'mynnised'. English omits Cumque nocte proxima illum rediturum ex verbis illius percepisset, struit insidias.

[258] H. & S. 'habergeam.'

[259] Ms. abbreviated form should be read 'perced' not 'parted,' as H. & S.; Lat. ut eo perforato eciam socium parum sauciaret.

[260] H. & S. 'changeable.'

[261] H. & S. read 'furnons,' but the Ms. form looks more like 'fumous' or 'fumons;' the corresponding Ms. reading in the Latin (I, 69, l. 42) is uestita instita uestis frunona, amended by H. & S. to read, vestita astuta vestis furnonae.

[262] H. & S. 'not.'

away and] for his infinite dreede rewarded with grete mede. Of whiche particioun made with his felaw he now hymsilf eftsoones no more swore.

Than he sorowful the hurt and damage of his possessioun and forsoth more sorowful the losse of his wif with the advowtrier[263] arraied to his felaw and felawesse as to the advowterer and advowteresse. [He] made forsoth an habundaunt and a plentivous felawship and feste, brought in and bad of his neighburghs and of his parentis and affinites, closed behynde the curteyn of the wif and his felaw replete and drunke, asked of hym if it pleased hym vnder guyle to Reherce and tel to the delectacioun of theym at the feste how moche money and in what maner he withdrow it from hir with whom he dide thadvowtry. Thadvowtrer deceived bi moche praier[264] and drynk reherced the thyng. And whan in thende of the Recreacioun of the mete the spirit of hym to moche bolned and stopped as often is don, as he drow the curteyn accised and bounden sigh and with turmentis; ther turned to hymsilf to thende of lesyng that sumwhat that he had told seemed to be of lesyng, saieng: "Whan and that other fested it was seen to me to stonde in thentre of a brage; and lo alsodainly the thunder seemed to be quasshed and broken, and whan I in al the violence with dreede fallyng of the horrible brak out of sleepe." And so of temporal thyng don turned the trowth in to fals fantasy and saved that he had almost lost. And vttirly[265] put his felawe in perdicioun and lost was wher that he covenaunted with an oth to depose al envie from his wif. With reconsiliacioun so made, she ordeyned newe guyles and wrenches of advowtrie. Whan he forsoth of that counsail the house fallen and broken of a poore man to his house a litel straite way she perced[266] under erth from that (f. 137) oon[267] house into that other[268] and had his free comyng and goyng whan that he wold. And whan this sufficed nat to theym, they toguyder saiden as to bien felawshipped in weddyng and Matremony and articulerly in thiese wordis:[269] "Mi lord is thi felaw; say thow to hym forwhi thow camst from thi cuntrey in wifes right and forwhi

---

[263] H. & S. 'advowterer.'

[264] H. & S. 'prier.' but the Ms. abbreviation would easily resolve into 'praier;' the Latin has Deceptus ille prece nima. This sentence inserted on lower margin of Ms.

[265] H. & S. 'vtterly.'

[266] H. & S. 'parted'; Lat. (I 70, l. 35) perforat.

[267] Omitted by H. & S.

[268] The translator missed the meaning of this sentence entirely, Cum enim ille ex illius consilio domum emisset a paupere domni sui socii contiguam, subterraneam perforat ille viam de domo in aliam.

[269] H. & S. 'woordis.'

that it is yowr maner and Saracyns lawe nat as to take a wif[270] but of the yift of a lawful man. Wiltow have hir of hym and of his yift as that thow hast nonother friend in this cuntrey? Whiche whan he seeth me shal trowe to be his and shal doubte. Than if that he turne hom as to see whether it be I, I shal meete and abide hym in the chamber;[271] [he] shal arbiter hymsilf to [be] disceived, than he turneth ageyn to the. And I eftsoones[272] shal come bifore hym, and so shal he yeve me to the to be seen of al theym that standen aboute; and so was it don."

XXIX. THE ROMAN MERCHANT WHO LAID A WAGER ON HIS WIFE'S CHASTITY.[273]

Ther were ii manchauntis in Rome of the whiche that oon had a wif, a chast[274] and a faire womman. Forsoth that other no trustifeith had in no womman. Whan and wherfor sumtyme whan and other wern disceived of wymmens[275] lightnes[276] he joied[277]; he forsoth of the trust and feith of his wif ageynsaide that other, of the whiche thei[278] put in plegge al their possessioun: this that he shuld corrupt hir withyn xv daies, he forwhi as with this condicioun stidefastly kept: that the husbond shuld nat warne or tel his wif of this covenaunt. She therfor busied with al maner of lightnes as with nothyng lad nor huyred, bi hir footemayde or seruaunt with yiftes corrupt she was disceived. Forsoth she had a Ryng that is to of hir first husbondes yift[279] above al possessiouns most diere.[280] She had also a vernacle[281] in signe and of an hand and an half from the kne vnto the Right hipe. And whan so bi the footemaide or seruaunt prively had taken he that knowen Ryng, and with the knowlache that I have saide, told and rehersed to his felaw as signes and tokenes of most certayne advowtrye, he bitake with cursid suspeccioun exiled hymsilf of his possessioun and vsid of exile. This

---

[270] H. & S. 'wit;' Lat. (I, 70, l. 42), coniugem.

[271] English omits first clause of next sentence, ubi cum invenerit me, when he has found me there.

[272] H. & S. 'eftscones.'

[273] See Mod. Lang. Notes, vol. XXIV, p. 219; H. & S., I, 71-72.

[274] H. & S. 'chaste.'

[275] H. & S. 'wymmenis.'

[276] 'lightnes' inserted on margin of Ms.

[277] H. & S. omit 'he joied.'

[278] H. & S. 'the.'

[279] Lat. (I, 71, l. 19) Habebat autem anulum sibi primum mariti manus. When this tale was printed in Mod. Lang. Notes several years ago (1909), the Latin original had not been published. For this reason I offer there a few emendations of the Middle English text; with the Latin text now accessible, my emendations are, for the most part, omitted in this reprint.

[280] H. & S. 'kiere'. Lat. carum (I, 71, l. 21.)

[281] Lat. verrucam.

thyng noised bi the Citee, she was outcast as advowteres and to the nephew or cosyn[282] of hir husbond she was committed.

Thei cam in to Alisaunder, and covered and hid with strength and kynde of clothis; beryng hymsilf evene to the kyng in manyfold seruice, in the friendship of the kyng hym bare as myght be in curtesye most swift and light. As admynistratrice of al the Realme the kynges Rentis wern infinytily multiplied bi his providence. Than themperour of Rome dede; his yong sone whan he Empired in the (f. 137b) Empire, herd of the sapient wisdam[283] of hym of Alisaunder, sent hym to Rome. [He] peased thempire, Restored soft and easy lawes in to the friendship of themperour and the Citezeins and the provynce with his high merites, nat puttyng hymsilf any symulacioun or token vnto his traitour. Bi hap and fortune [she] fond hir husbond among poore folk most porest and dide hym to be nurisshed. And bifore his traitour dide to be Rehersed his treason bifore the Citezeyns; that don arraied a feste to the delectacioun that is to say of felawship and festers; than at the last he opened and deemed into deth of his owne confessioun. The pore man went his wey and she to hir husbond.

XXX. The Unchaste Wife and the Rescue of Her Lover

Svche on willyng to chastice his nephew or Cosyn and to withdrawe hym from the vnlieful love of wymmen and from the vnnumerable aduersities whiche often tyme fallith of this vnhappy thyng, of suche a clerk dide to write the pavour, basshidnes, and the dreede.

Svche a myghti man ther was[284] whiche suche a day from his house the space of a daies jorney went to his place. The wif forsoth for hir housbondis made sure suche a clerk hir love, cald [hym] in the derk of the nyght. Whiche while of the fowle lust that thei vsiden, the husbonde vnavised and vnwares com hom ageyne. Forsoth ther mette hym in his jorney [oon] whiche plesaunt thynges hym told. To whom al his houshold meyne mette hym with lightis. The clerk heryng that wherfor to torn hym vttirly[285] he wist nat. Only out of the chamber he[286] went for to huyde hym and for overmoche dreede so astonyed that he wist nat wher to torne hym, or bi what wey to go out of the Court vttirly[287] he wist nat.

---

[282] Lat. nepos.
[283] H. & S. 'wisdom.'
[284] English omits babens uxorem.
[285] H. & S. 'vtterley.'
[286] H. & S. 'hee.'
[287] H. & S. 'vtterly.'

Forsoth also he herd al the houshold as in suche a busynes evene moeved, and to tho thynges whiche to the lord and his felawship and to hors wern necessary, here and ther ran and arraied. In the meane while the wikked wif was so gnawen in hir conscience for dreede lest she shuld be take with the clerk, mette hir husbond with faire delicious wordis that he shulde nat be suspect of hir cursed deedis, willyng if that she myght nat only hym, but al his felawship in like gladnes, lest anything with grace issued withoutfurth as only the cause of his so soone comyng to require, she beyng glad in as moche as she myght to withhold as to shewe agenst a friend. The wretchid clerk huydeng[288] in a corner for the dreede of the houshold meyne til al wern housed, was nat so hardy to go out of the Court. Forsoth he knew hymsilf to be prived of his life if he at suche tyme he wer ther founde of any of the lordes (f. 138) meyne. Whiche put and sette in so straite[289] an angwissh, seeyng nowher no subsidie, refuge, nor help whider to flee, sawe a Tonne of the whiche that on end was out, lay in the porche of the house. The whiche forsoth whan he had seen, thider tended, and willyng hymsilf ther to huyde, entred in hopyng to escape the perel folowyng. But with the maner of that fere and basshidnes his drede bigan to augmente and to encrease. Forwhi ther was a Bere tied in the Court the whiche brak his cheyne at the discours and rennyng of the servauntis[290] whom the houndis foloweden hider and thider and in their pursute hym bote and driew, and of veray neede coarted hym to entre in to the Tonne above saide. The meyne and seruauntis fallyng to with grete and stavis willyng to drawe hym out, myght nat performe it, whos body was al hid save only the hede. The grace of this maner thyng of theym withoutfurth expelleden ran to that other part of the tonne to cast out the bottum. The wretche whiche was hid withyn tremblyng, quakyng and wailyng, praieng god that thei myght nat breke it, hield fast with al his myght, and with his feete knocked and smote on the Beres bak and with his hede he hield the bottum; so the Bere wold he nold he fled and the wretche huydyng remayned. The suters of this thyng ne bien thei nat of this vnremembred.

---

[288] H. & S. 'huyding.'

[289] H. & S. 'sofraite'!

[290] Not in the Latin: Quem canes insectantes, hac illacque sequentes et morsibus attrectantes. I, 73, 11. 20-22.

Wm. Ramsdell, Son & Co.

GROCERS

10551 Euclid Avenue